"THE LADY LUCK"

Story of the USS LST-864

by

Mike Martin

THE FOWBLE PRESS

SEPTEMBER, 2021

⊰ PUBLICATION DATA ⊱

PUBLISHER:	Published in the United States of America by The Fowble Press
COPYRIGHT:	© 2021 by Mickey J. "Mike" Martin
ISBN:	SECOND EDITION ISBN 9781737140603
LCCN:	2021916527
RIGHTS:	Contact Mickey J. "Mike" Martin THE FOWBLE PRESS 25455 Fossa Drive Tomball, Texas 77375

⊰ ⊱

❧ DEDICATION ☙

This book is dedicated to Elmer Porter, who was killed in action in the South Pacific on November 1, 1944, during World War II. Born in Hoffman, Oklahoma, he served on the USS Suwannee. He was first my father's childhood friend and then, later, a relative by marriage. May God bless him and all other young men just like him who have given up their lives in defense of our country.

"War is an ugly thing, but not the ugliest thing: the decayed and degraded state of moral and patriotic feeling which thinks nothing worth a war is worse . . . a man who has nothing which he cares about more than his personal safety is a miserable creature who has no chance of being free, unless made and kept so by the exertions of better men than himself." John Stewart Mill.

❧ ☙

CONTENTS

1	Wartime Launch of the USS LST-864	11
2	Officers and Crews of LST-864	19
	Officers of the First Crew	20
	First Crew	21
	Officers of the Second Crew	26
	Second Crew	27
3	The Lady Luck	83
4	The Lady Luck at War	89
	Wartime Message from Captain to Crew	89
	The "Scuttlebutt"	131
5	War Diary of LST Group Ninety-One	151
6	History of the U.S.S. LST-864	177
7	Wartime Memories of Captain Richard B. Wathen	189
8	Reunions of LST-864 Shipmates	213
9	Thanks for a Job Well Done	245
	INDEX	261

"THE LADY LUCK"

Story of the U.S.S. LST-864

By

Mickey J. "Mike" Martin

CHAPTER 1

WARTIME LAUNCH OF THE USS LST-864

Landing Ships--Tanks, or LSTs, were United States Navy vessels especially designed to transport military equipment and troops in support of Allied involvement in World War II. Jokingly referred to by crewmen as "Large, Slow Targets" due to their being notoriously rough riding at sea and relatively lightly armed, they nevertheless performed an essential and invaluable role throughout the conflict. They were the workhorses of the war, carrying troops, supplies and equipment to wherever they were needed.

The design and functionality of these ships was refined through experiments conducted at a facility constructed for this specific purpose. Straightforwardly called "The LST Building," it replicated every detail of the tank deck of an LST Ship, including replication of interior girders and rivets. Details of the upper deck of an LST Ship, such as the railing and pilot house, also were replicated. Since the tank deck rides below water level on these ships, the building originally had no windows--these were not added until later on, after it was turned into a classroom. In addition to the experiments that were conducted in the building, many troops received training in embarkation and debarkation techniques there as well.

The work that was done in the LST Building resulted in many design modifications of the LST Ships, all of which increased its effectiveness and safety for the transportation of tens of thousands of troops and untold tons of equipment during World War II. As a result, in 1998 it was determined eligible for listing on the National Register of Historic Places. The LST Building was a truly unique facility, an example of early joint forces' operations--the Army, Navy, and British Admiralty contributed to its design, construction, and use.

Since the 1970's, the LST Building has been used to store antique tanks. The interesting photograph of it that follows was provided by Charlie Ridenour in the Fall/Winter, 2000-2001edition (Volume XI, Number 2, Pages 9-10) of "*Bitts & Pieces,*" the Newsletter of the Howard Steamboat Museum.

The USS LST-864, one of a large number LSTs, was launched on November 18, 1944, at the "Jeffboat" shipyards in Jeffersonville, Indiana. It was sponsored, or christened, by Mrs. Viola J. Wathen, a resident of the city and the wife of its first captain. The ship departed from the site of its construction and launching on December 7, 1944, but it was not formally commissioned for service in the Pacific until December 13 of that same year.

From Jeffersonville, Indiana, the ship was taken down the river to New Orleans, after making a short stop in Memphis along the way. Additional finishing work was done in New Orleans, including fitting it with guns on its bow and stern. When the final fitting was completed, it was taken to Panama City, Florida, as a shakedown cruise. During this period, the crew practiced the procedures of landing and retraction under simulated battle conditions.

The USS LST-864 finally went to sea on January 16, 1945. It passed through the Panama Canal and up the West Coast to San Diego and eventually on to Seattle. After being loaded with equipment and a company of Army Aviation Engineers assigned to participate in the invasion of Okinawa, the ship steamed off into the Pacific to join the war in earnest.

It is only by happenstance that there is a good photographic record of the ship's activities during the war, since picture taking was for the most part a rather haphazard and unplanned activity. In the first place, it was a court martial offense to be caught taking certain kinds of pictures, out of fear that even the most innocent and personal of photographs might fall into the wrong hands and thereby unintentionally end up becoming detrimental to the war effort or to the reputation or image of the United States Navy. On numerous occasions the skipper warned the crew that anyone caught taking pictures of the ship would be punished, which led some of the men to avoid the activity altogether.

Sailors, however, didn't always strictly abide by this prohibition; they took photographs for their own use whenever they were on leave or in port or at play. Even though they did not have the best of equipment and were not particularly skilled as photographers, the activities they recorded in bits and snatches along the way made this book possible. In combination, they create a wonderful pictorial record. Their innocent photographs did not compromise the security or the mission of the ship in any way. Combined as they are in this book, they form a priceless memento that we can all enjoy today.

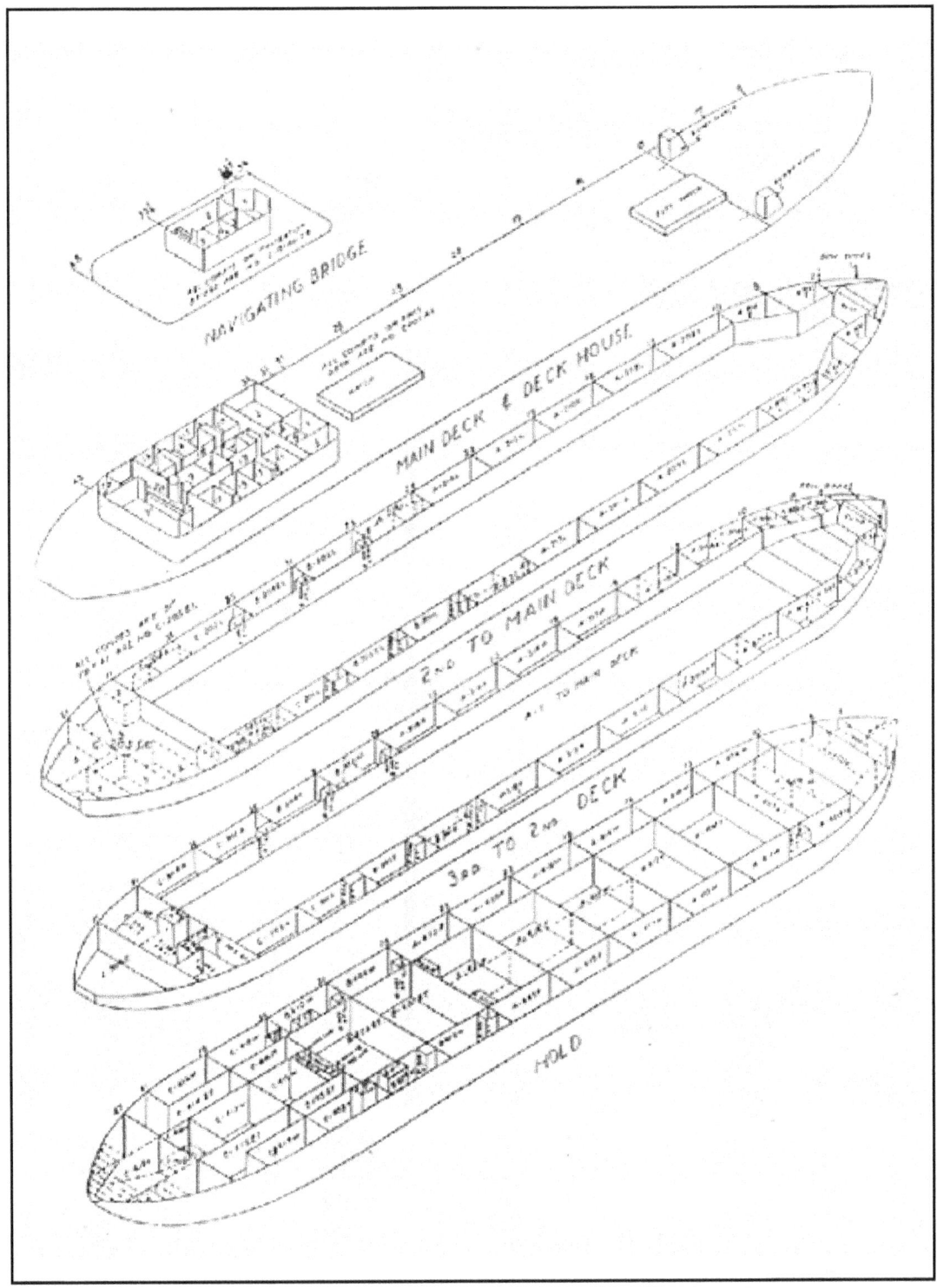

LST Hull Schematic, Jeff Boat and Machine Company, Inc., Jeffersonville, Indiana

LST Research and Training Facility at Fort Knox, Kentucky

Crewmen at Jeffersonville, Indiana, shipyard location, waiting to board the USS LST-864

Christening of the USS LST-864 by Mrs. Viola Wathen on November 18, 1944, at Jeffersonville, Indiana

LAUNCHING OF THE USS LST-864
Jeffersonville, Indiana, on November 19, 1944

The USS LST-864 in the Panama Canal

LST-864 officers and crew standing for inspection in San Francisco

*LST Advanced Basic Training on Beach #1205
at Camp Bradford, Virginia*

LST BASIC TRAINING CLASS
(Robert Martin – Second Row from front, second from left.)

Aerial view of the USS LST-864, fully loaded
and headed out to join the war in the Pacific

CHAPTER 2

OFFICERS AND CREWS OF THE USS LST-864

A staff of 10 officers and up to 100 seamen manned the USS LST-864. The first crew was assembled by taking men on board at various points along the way between the shipyard in Jeffersonville, Indiana, where the ship was constructed and launched at its point of departure for the Panama Canal at Panama City, Florida.

Only two teams of officers and crewmen staffed the ship before she was taken out of military service at the end of the war. Although some officers and men served on both crews, since those days officers and men alike have referred to serving as members of "the first crew" or "the second crew," or on both. As many pictures as could be located are included in the pages that follow. Some of them are copies of copies, but, unfortunately, they were all that were available.

Young men from all parts of the country were brought in to serve on LST-864, many after being drafted or otherwise signing up "for the duration" of the war. In the same way that ships were constructed in a hurry during the wartime emergency, officers were trained in a hurry as well. That's why they were often referred to as "Ninety Day Wonders." Crewmen were trained in even more of a hurry, many of them signing on with almost no training or practical experience at all. The average crewman was 21 years and 6 months old, and the first commander of the ship, Captain Richard B. Wathen, was only 27 years of age himself. Captain Wathen had only two years of combat experience, and only five members of his crew had ever been to sea. Most of the crew had only about six weeks of advance training before coming on board; the rest of their training was delivered on the job. The commander of the second crew was C. R. Grady.

NAVPERS—136 (REV. 1-44)		DECK LOG—LIST OF OFFICERS		CONFIDENTIAL

LIST OF OFFICERS ATTACHED TO AND ON BOARD THE U.S.S. **L. S. T. 864**, COMMANDED BY **Richard B. Wathen, Lieutenant** U.S.N.R., DURING THE PERIOD COVERED BY THIS LOG BOOK, WITH DATE OF REPORTING FOR DUTY, DETACHMENT, OR DEATH, FROM **1 July**, 19 **45**, TO **31 July**, 19 **45**

NAME AND FILE NUMBER (Show file No. below name)	RANK	DATE OF REPORTING ON BOARD / DATE OF DETACHMENT (Show detachment date below reporting date)	PRIMARY DUTIES	NAME, RELATIONSHIP, AND ADDRESS OF NEXT OF KIN (Show address at which BuPers may most readily communicate with next of kin in an emergency)
R. B. Wathen 151986	Lieut.	13 Dec. 44	Commanding Officer.	Wife – Mrs. Viola James Wathen, 260 Cherokee Road, Charlotte, N.C.
F. L. Haines 389616	Ens.	13 Dec. 44	Executive Officer.	Mother – Mabel Andrew Haines 315 E. Center, Blanchester, Ohio
J. W. Holland 401753	Ens.	13 Dec. 44	First Lieutenant.	Wife – Mrs. Phyllis Barlow Holland Bombay, New York, Box 95.
R. D. Peter Jr. 353645	Ens.	13 Dec. 44	Engineering Officer.	Wife – Mrs. Dora Mae C. Peter R. D. #1, Norristown, Panna.
L. P. Holmes Jr. 370706	Ens.	13 Dec. 44	Communications Officer.	Father – Llewellyn P. Holmes Sr. P.O. Box 35, Napa, Calif.
W. R. Hanley 371056	Ens.	13 Dec. 44	Stores Officer.	Father – William D. Hanley 3986 Murdock Ave. NYC, New York
E. P. Hanley 371055	Ens.	13 Dec. 44	Gunnery Officer.	Mother – Della Coughlin Hanley 3986 Murdock Ave. NYC, New York
P. N. Wood 340350	Ens.	13 Dec. 44	Assistant Executive Officer.	Mother – Hannie Elizabeth Wood Douglasville, Ga.
B. W. Gibson 360357	Ens.	13 Dec. 44	Assistant First Lieutenant.	Mother – Lottie Monette Gibson Box #8, Seminary, Mississippi.

EXAMINED AND FOUND TO BE CORRECT:

Ens F. L. Haines U.S.N. NAVIGATOR.

TO BE FORWARDED DIRECT TO THE BUREAU OF NAVAL PERSONNEL AT THE END OF EACH MONTH

OFFICERS OF THE FIRST CREW OF THE USS LST-864

FIRST CREW
USS LST-864 -- THE LADY LUCK

1. Abderhalden, Ernest William
2. Adair, Richard Gale
3. Adams, Charles Omer
4. Adams, Harley Lee
5. Alegarode, Sydney Cordell
6. Bailey, Howard
7. Barrow, William Bruce Jr.
8. Bartlett, Delmare Filmore
9. Bauer, Merle Floyd
10. Bausman, Harold Lee
11. Belcher, Donald Arthur
12. Belding, Croy Eugene
13. Bell, Robert Louis
14. Bell, Walter Clarence
15. Benoit, Leon George
16. Berry, Thomas Willard
17. Bertouille, Walter Edward
18. Berzinski, Roman August
19. Bittiker, Harold Gene
20. Broward, Montcalm III
21. Brown, Charles Albert
22. Brown, Guile Fray
23. Buckingham, James Robert
24. Bunker, Frank
25. Charbless, Eugene
26. Cleary, William Warner
27. Collier, Vernon
28. Crowell, Edward Belchner
29. Cruchfield, Fry Dovett Sr.
30. Cummins, Samuel Martin
31. Denton, Jack Walton
32. Deyer, Hugh Patrick
33. DiPalma, Andy
34. Dismon, John Bedford
35. Dobes, Frank William
36. Dobesh, Joseph George
37. Dukman, Jerry Marvin Jr.
38. Ellis, David Nelson
39. Emmel, Donald John
40. Evans, James Haldon
41. Femrack, John Phillip
42. Flatt, Savage Dyer
43. Fry, Ernest Abraham
44. Gainor, John Paul
45. Gay, David
46. Gregg, Robert Leonard Jr.
47. Guida, Arthur Joseph
48. Hammond, John Glenn
49. Harmon, Arthur Ross
50. Hock, Erwin Arthur
51. Hogle, Paul Arnold
52. Holmes, James Richard
53. Horner, Lewis Clinton
54. Hughlin, James Hiram
55. Jacobson, Carlo Martin
56. Jensen, Harry Martin Sr.
57. Kaehler, Malcolm Andrew
58. Knutson, Arthur Carl
59. Langhett, Gerald LeRoy
60. Lapham, Marvin James

61. Larkin, Charles Francis
62. Lawson, Romma Junior
63. Levertee, Garland Harold
64. Lipinski, James Victor
65. Loar, Paul David
66. Lyon, Malcolm Bernard
67. Magel, Sal M.
68. Maher, John
69. May, Normal Call
70. Marshall, Jesse Ray
71. Martin, Robert Jackson
72. McCloud, Nathanial
73. Merriman, Lowall Arthur
74. Miller, Ronald Boyd
75. Mitchell, Robart
76. Mockbridge, Joseph Aleck
77. Mueller, William Joseph
81. Mullen, John Herman
79. Murray, Lawrence Ralph
80. Myers, Herbert Benjamin
81. Neal, Jack Lloyd
82. O'Brien, Byron Francis
83. Parker, Ralph Wilbert
84. Parrick, LeRoy Junior
85. Paulik, Joseph James
86. Perry, Elderidge
87. Pitts, Issac Newton Jr.
88. Plonka, Alaxander
89. Prokop, Andrew
90. Provins, William Robert
91. Reeble, William Keller Jr.
92. Regel, Robert Christopher
93. Robins, William Hamilton
94. Rose, Glen Oval
95. Rose (or Ross), Richard Claude
96. Rushing, Walter O.
97. Russell, Rodger Webb
98. Satterly, Lillard S.
99. Schuler, Albert Joseph
100. Shelton, James M.
101. Sowder, Jess
102. Storgaard, Chester Helm
103. Stotts, Emery Eugene
104. Swazey, Leanard Willis
105. Swope, Julius Harold
106. Terry, Joe Alexander
107. Thomas, Walter Evans
108. Thompson, Thurman N.
109. Tinlin, Hubert Orton
110. Truesdale, Vister Rutledge Jr.
111. Walczak, Leonard
112. Whitehead, Clovie Armon
113. Wick, Leander Norvert
114. Winters, Charles Grandt
115. Wolbach, Paul Walter
116. Womack, James Hubert

NOTE: Lists like this one are often inaccurate and incomplete, since men were constantly coming and going from the ship. John Maher, for example, was a member of the first crew who boarded at Seattle, Washington, on February 20, 1945, before the ship went overseas on February 26, 1945. He left the ship for discharge in May of 1946.

OFFICERS AND CREW OF THE USS LST-864

Ensign F. Lee Haines

Ensign P. N. Wood

Chiefs William Robert Provins and Walter O. Rushing

Charles O. (or Harley L.) Adams and Joe Dobesh (left) in the equipment room

Unnamed and Issac Newton Pitts in the Electrical Shop

Walter Thomas (Right) and Joe Dobesh in the Equipment Room

Herbert B. Myers with parents Walter and Anne just prior to induction

Herbert B. Myers leaving home for induction

Herbert B. Myers being seen off to war

Herbert B. Myers home on leave from training

U.S.S. LST-864
OFFICERS OF THE SECOND CREW

NAVPERS-136 (REV. 1-44)   DECK LOG—LIST OF OFFICERS   CONFIDENTIAL

LIST OF OFFICERS ATTACHED TO AND ON BOARD THE U.S.S. **L.S.T. 864**, COMMANDED BY **C.R. Grady Lt. (jg)** U.S.N.R., DURING THE PERIOD COVERED BY THIS LOG BOOK, WITH DATE OF REPORTING FOR DUTY, DETACHMENT, OR DEATH, FROM **1 December**, 1945, TO **31 December**, 1945.

NAME AND FILE NUMBER (Show file No. below name)	RANK	DATE OF REPORTING ON BOARD / DATE OF DETACHMENT (Show detachment date below reporting date)	PRIMARY DUTIES	NAME, RELATIONSHIP AND ADDRESS OF NEXT OF KIN (Show address at which BuPers may most readily communicate with next of kin in an emergency)
Haines, F.L. 389616	Ensign	13 Dec. 44 / 22 Dec. 45	Commanding Officer	Mother-Mabel Andrew Haines 315 E. Center, Blanchester, Ohio
Williams, J.W. 309699	Lt.(jg)	22 Dec. 45 / 27 Dec. 45	Commanding Officer	Wife-Mrs. J.L. Williams 930 SCott Street San Francisco, Calif.
Grady, C.R. 312108	Lt. (jg)	23 Dec. 45	Commanding Officer	Mother-Mrs Grady Big Timber, Montana
Holland, J.W. 401753	Ensign	13 Dec. 44	Executive Officer.	Wife-Mrs Pyllis Barlow Holland Bombay, New York, Box 95
Peter, R.D. Jr. 353645	Lt.(jg)	13 Dec. 44 / 5 Dec. 45	Executive Officer	Wife-Mrs Dora Mae C. Peter R.D. 1, Norristown, Penn.
Gibson, B.W. 360357	Ensign	13 Dec. 44	First Lieutenant	Mother- Lottie Monette Gibson Box.8, Seminary, Mississippi
Wood, P.N. 340350	Ensign	13 Dec. 44	Engineering Officer	Mother- Hannie Elizabeth Wood Douglasville, Ga.
Holmes, L.P. Jr. 370706	Ensign	13 Dec. 44	Communication Officer	Father-Llewellyn P. Holmes Sr. P.O. Box 35, Napa, California
Hanley, W.R. 371055	Ensign	13 Dec. 44 / 5 Dec. 45	Stores Officer	Father-William D. Hanley 3986 Murdock Ave., NYC, New York
Hanley, E.P. 371056	Ensign	13 Dec. 44 / 5 Dec. 45	Gunnery Officer	Mother-Della Coughlin Hanley 3986 Murdock Ave., NYC, New York

EXAMINED AND FOUND TO BE CORRECT:

J.W. Holland U.S.N.R. NAVIGATOR.

TO BE FORWARDED DIRECT TO THE BUREAU OF NAVAL PERSONNEL AT THE END OF EACH MONTH

OFFICERS OF THE SECOND CREW OF THE USS LST-864

SECOND CREW
USS LST-864 -- THE LADY LUCK

1. Adams, Charles
2. Allen, James D.
3. Andrews, Fred C.
4. Ashton, Donald D.
5. Babineaux, Salamon
6. Baerlin, Elmer E.
7. Berman, Rayman M.
8. Barnes, Archie L.
9. Bellis, Merle L.
10. Berry, Francis T.
11. Browder, Robert W.
12. Bower, Floyd J.
13. Branch, Eugene M.
14. Brandmair, Wilbur F.
15. Burns, Francis J.
16. Caldie, John P.
16. Cari, Robert R.
17. Carlascio, William
18. Carlton, Burnis P.
19. Dobesh, Joseph G.
20. Dorl, John R.
21. Evans, James H.
22. Ferguson, Frank L.
23. Ferrell, James M.
24. Furnweger, Alfred J.
25. Granberry, Henery L.
26. Harp, Tea Jr.
27. Jewell, Claude E.
28. Keeler, Raymond E.
29. Kidd, Frank C.
30. Lachey, Bruce N.
31. Largent, Charles W.
32. Leake, John G.
33. Lewis, Willie
34. Majors, Charlie O.
35. Martinez, Salvador
36. Michel, Willie J.
37. Mosier, Milton Jr.
38. Novak, Joseph
39. Ostrem, Richard W.
40. Page, Thomas A.
41. Phillips, Richard
42. Porter, Norman L.
43. Reed, William M.
44. Rogers, Richard F.
45. Russell, Humphrey G.
46. Smith, Kenneth L.
47. Smith, Richard F.
48. Smolich, George
49. Tavron, M. C.
50. Taylor, Robert V.
51. Thompson, Willie L.
52. Thurgo, Lyle E.
53. Walling, John W.
54. Warren, William K.
55. White, Ova C. Jr.
56. Wilder, J. W. Jr.
57. Williams, John J.
58. Wilson, William B.

POWER OF ATTORNEY

General

KNOW ALL MEN BY THESE PRESENTS: That I, John Paul Gainor a legal reisdent of 409 Chestnut St. Coatesville, Pa. Now in the naval service as a F1c, service as a F1c, service No. 920-88-17 USNR, in the service of the United States, and anticipating that a Power of Attorney may be useful in certain circumstances, have made, constituted and appointed and by these presents do mke, constitute and appoint Sarah Harrison Gainor, whose address is 409 Chestnut St. Coatesville, Pa. my true and lawful attorney to act in manage, and conduct all my estate and all my affairs and for that purpose, for men and in my name, place, and stead, and for my use and benefit, and as my act and deed, to do and execute, or to concur with persons jointly interested with myseld there in the doing or excution of, all or any the following acts, deeds, and things, that is to say;
(1) To buy, receive, lease, accept, or otherwise acquire; to sell, convey mortgage, hypothecate, pledge, quit claim or otherwise encumber or dispose of; or to contract to agree for the acquisition, disposal, or encumbrance, of; any property whatsoever or any custody, pessession, interest, or right therein, upon such terms as my said attorney shall thick proper; (2) To take, hold, possess, invest, lease, or let, or otherwise manage any or all of my property of any interest therein; to eject, remove, or relieve tenants or other persons from, and recover possession of, such property by all lawful means; and to maintain, protect, preserve, insure, remove, store, transport, repair, rebuild, modify, or improve the same or any part thereof; (3) To make, do, and transact all and every kind of business of what nature or kind soever, including the receipt, recovery, collection, payment, compromise, settlement, and adjustment of all accounts, legacies, bequests, interests, dividends, annuities, demands, dibts, owing, or payable by me or to me; (4) To make, bonds, indorse, accept receive, sign, seal, execute, acknowledge checks, notes, bonds, vouchers, receipts, and such other instruments, in writing of whatever kind and nature as may be necessary, convenient, or proper in the premisess; (5) To deposit and withdraw for the purposes hereof, in either my said attorney's name or my name or jointly in both our names, in or from any banking institution, any funds, negotiable paper, or moneys which may come into my said attorney's hands as such attorney or which I now or hereafter may have on deposit or be entitled to; (6) To institute, prosecute, defend, compromise, arbitrate, and dispose of lefal, equitable, ro administrative hearings, actions, suits, attachments, arrest, distresses to other proceedings, or otherwise engage in litigation in connection with the premises;
(7) To act as my attorney or proxy in respect to any stocks, shares bonds or other investments, rights, to interests, I may now or hereafter hold;

Page 1 of Power of attorney prepared aboard ship for seaman John Paul "Pops" Gainor and notarized by Ensign Philip N. Wood

(8) To ingage and dismiss agents, counsel, and employees, and to appoint and remove to appoint and remove at pleasure any substitute for, or agent of my said attorney in respect to all or any of the matters or things herein mentioned and upon such terms as my attorney, shall think fit.

(9) To execute vouchers in my befalf for any and all allowances and reimbursements properly payable to hold effects as authorized by law or navy regulations, and to receive, indorse, and collect the proceeds of checks payable to the order of the undersigned drawn on the Treasurer of the United States; (10) To take reports, applications, requests and documents; (11) To take possession, and order the removal and shipment, of any of my property from any post, warehouse, depot, dock or other place of storage or safekeeping, governmental or private; and to execute and deliver any release, vouchers, receipt, shipping ticket, certificate, or other instrument necessary or convenient for such purpose.

GIVING AND GRANTING unto mh said attorney full power and authority to do and perform all and every act, deed, matter, and thing effectually to all intents and purposes as I might or could do in my own proper person if personally present, the above specially enumerated powers being in aid and exmplification of the full, conplete, and general power herein granted and not in limitation or definition thereof; and hereby ratifying all that my said attorney shall lawfully do or cause to be done by virtue of these presents.

And I hereby declare that any act or thing lawfully done hereunder by my said attorney shall be binding on myself, and my heirs, legal and personal representative, and assigns whether the same shall have been done before or after my death, or other revocation of this instrument, unless and until reliable intelligence or notice thereof shall have been received by my said attorney; and whether or not I, the grantor of this instrument, shall have been reported or listed either officially or otherwise, as "missing in action" as that phrase is used in naval parlance, it being the intendment hereof that such status designation shall not bar my attorney from fully and completely exercising and continuing to exercise any and all powers and rights herein granted, and that such report of missing in action", shall neither constitute or be interpreted as constituting noice of my death nor operat to revoke this instrument.

IN WITNESS WHEREOF, I have hereunto set my hand and seal the 16 day of April, 1945

John Paul Gainor

Page 2 of Power of attorney prepared aboard ship for seaman John Paul "Pops" Gainor and notarized by Ensign Philip N. Wood

WITNESSES:

Hubert O. Sinlin   Charles F. Larkin
Saul A. Hoge   Darrell L Wever
Charles B. Winters   Walter E. Thomas

ACKNOWLEDGMENT

I, P. N. Wood, Ensign, USNR, do hereby certify, that I am a duly commissioned, qualified and authorized notary public in and for the U.S.S. L.S.T. 864; and that John Paul Gainor grantor in the foregoing power of Attorney, dated 16 April 1945 and hereto annexed, who is personally well known to me as the person who executed the fore-going Power od Attorney, appeared before me this day within the territorial limits of my authority, and being first duly sworn, executed said insttrument after the contents thereof had been read and duly explained to him, and acknowledge that the exection of said instrument by him was his free and voluntary act and deed for the uses and purpose therein set forth.

    In witness whereof, I have hereunto set my hand and affixed my official seal this 16 day of April 1945.

                                                        Philip N. Wood
                                                        Ens. USNR

Recorded in the Office for Recording of Deeds, &c, in and for Chester County Pennsylvania, in Letter of Attorney Book N-2, Vol. 38, Page 284, Witness my hand & Seal of Office this 26th day of July, Anno Domini 1945.
                                    Recorder of Deeds

7920.
John Paul Gainor
Sarah Harrison Gainor
Mrs John Gainor
409 Chestnut St
Coatesville, Pa

Page 3 of Power of attorney prepared aboard ship for Seaman John Paul "Pops" Gainor and notarized by Ensign Philip N. Wood. NOTE: Many sailors, having signed up for the duration of the war, had power of attorney documents drafted aboard ship in case they were killed in action. These documents were prepared by officers and witnessed by crewmates, as shown by this example.

Captain Richard B. Wathen on the Bridge

*Ensign
F. Lee Haines*

*Robert D. Peter Jr.
Engineering Officer 1*

MASCOTS ABOARD SHIP

The Lady Luck had two mascots, a dog named LST-864 and a monkey named Chi Chi. At least for a while, they were aboard at the same time. On occasions, Chi Chi would give LST-864 a lot of grief!

Twins W. R. "Bill" Hanley (Left), Stores Officer, and E. P. "Gene" Hanley, Gunnery Officer

Stores Officer Ensign W. R. "Bill" Hanley

Gunnery Officer E. P. "Gene" Hanley

*Ensign Phillip Newton "Newt" Wood,
Assistant Executive Officer and Personnel Officer*

*Officers McWhorter, Wood, Tamulwich, and Gibson
in the LST-864 Boardroom*

Engineering Officer Robert D. Peter, Jr.

Ensign J. W. Holland, Executive Officer – July of 1945. Ensign Holland became Executive Officer after Captain Wathen left as Officer of the Deck (OOD).

Issac Newton Pitts, Jr., S1cSK, in the ship's office, in a cloud of pipe smoke.

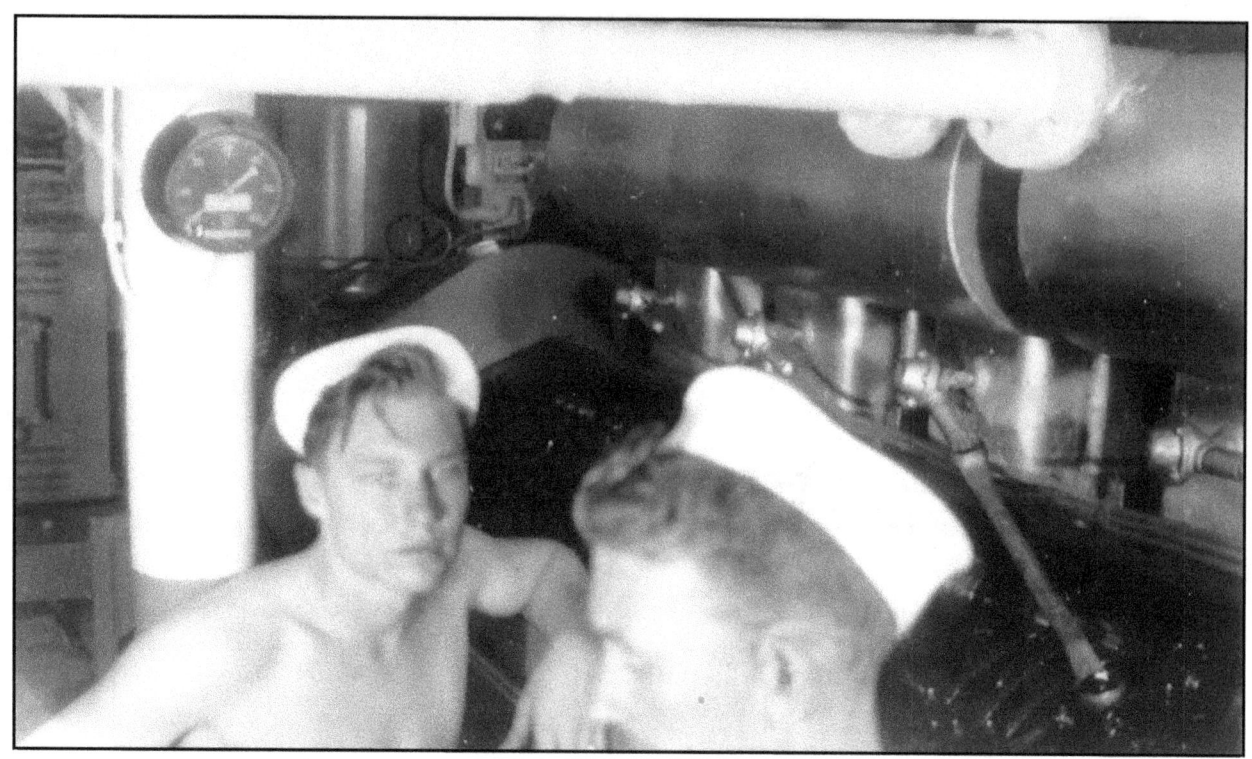

Carlo Martin Jacobsen (left) and Ova C. White, in the main engine room

Ova C. White, in the main engine room.

Carlo Jacobson, Harold Gene Bittaker, and Arthur Carl Knutson

Richard Claude Rose (or Ross) (left), Ensign F. L. Haines, Byron Francis O'Brien, and Joseph Paulik on Deck

Jack Denton *John R. Dorl* *James Ferraro*

Leonard Walczak (Welder) *Ernest A. Fry* *Frank Burns*

OFFICERS AND CREW OF THE USS LST-864

John Maher
MOMM 3/c

Marvin James
Lapham

Jack Lloyd Neal
MOMM 3/c

Art Knutson
MOMM 2/c

Richard Claude
Rose (or Ross)

John
Walling

Unnamed and Leonard Swazey on deck

Dave Ellis in whites, saluting

Howard E. "Buck" Bailey (left) and Frank Burns, "at their best!"

OFFICERS AND CREW OF THE USS LST-864

*Walter "Charles" Bell, Jr.
Boot Camp*

*Howard "Buck" Bailey
(right) and Unknown*

*"Rufe" (Left, Full Name
Unknown) and Howard
"Buck Bailey*

*Unknown
Sailor*

- 43 -

Joe Dobesh, William Warren, and John Walling on the deck

Officers and crewmen on the deck of LST-864

OFFICERS AND CREW OF THE USS LST-864

*Ova C. White on a
40MM gun at Okinawa*

*John Maher (left) and
John Walling in Hawaii*

View of the bow section of LST-864, fully loaded

- 45 -

Byron O'Brien, Harold Bausman, Thurman Thompson, Richard Adair, and James Holmes

Charles Adams, Unknown, Normal May, and Garland Leverett

OFFICERS AND CREW OF THE USS LST-864

Frank Dobes (Left), Merle Bauer (Center), and Unknown

Frank Dobes and Clint Horner

Name Unknown

"Finn" (Full Name Unknown)

"Sparky" (or "Spanky") (Full Name Unknown)

Jim Lipinski, David Gay, and Vister Truesdale

"Augie"
(Full Name Unknown)

"Zeke" (Nickname Uncertain)
(Full Name Unknown)

*Leonard Walczak, Chief Walter Rushing,
and an unidentified crewman*

*Frank Bunker (Left),
James Womack and Robert Martin*

Crewmen on Liberty. (Standing) - Paul Wolbach (Left), Unknown, and Unknown; (Kneeling) - Unknown, Unknown, Frank Bunker, and Robert Martin

Walter Bertouille, Leanard Swazey, and H. E. Bullington

Frank Burns (Left) and Leanard Swazey

William M. "Bill" Reed
Second Crew

Glen Oval "Rosie"
Rose

Howard E. "Buck" Bailey
and C. A. Utberg, Jr.

Robert Lewis
Bell

Cooks and bakers of LST-864. Robert Martin (top left at the back) and Frank Bunker (front row at center); other names unknown

PLAYING AROUND ABOARD THE SHIP
"Little Brown" (center) "shooting" Jack Denton. "Big Brown" (seated) and Robert Martin (in the right background).

Basketball players LeRoy Parrick, Jim Lipinski, Howard "Buck" Bailey, and unknown

Cooks Big Brown (left) and Little Brown

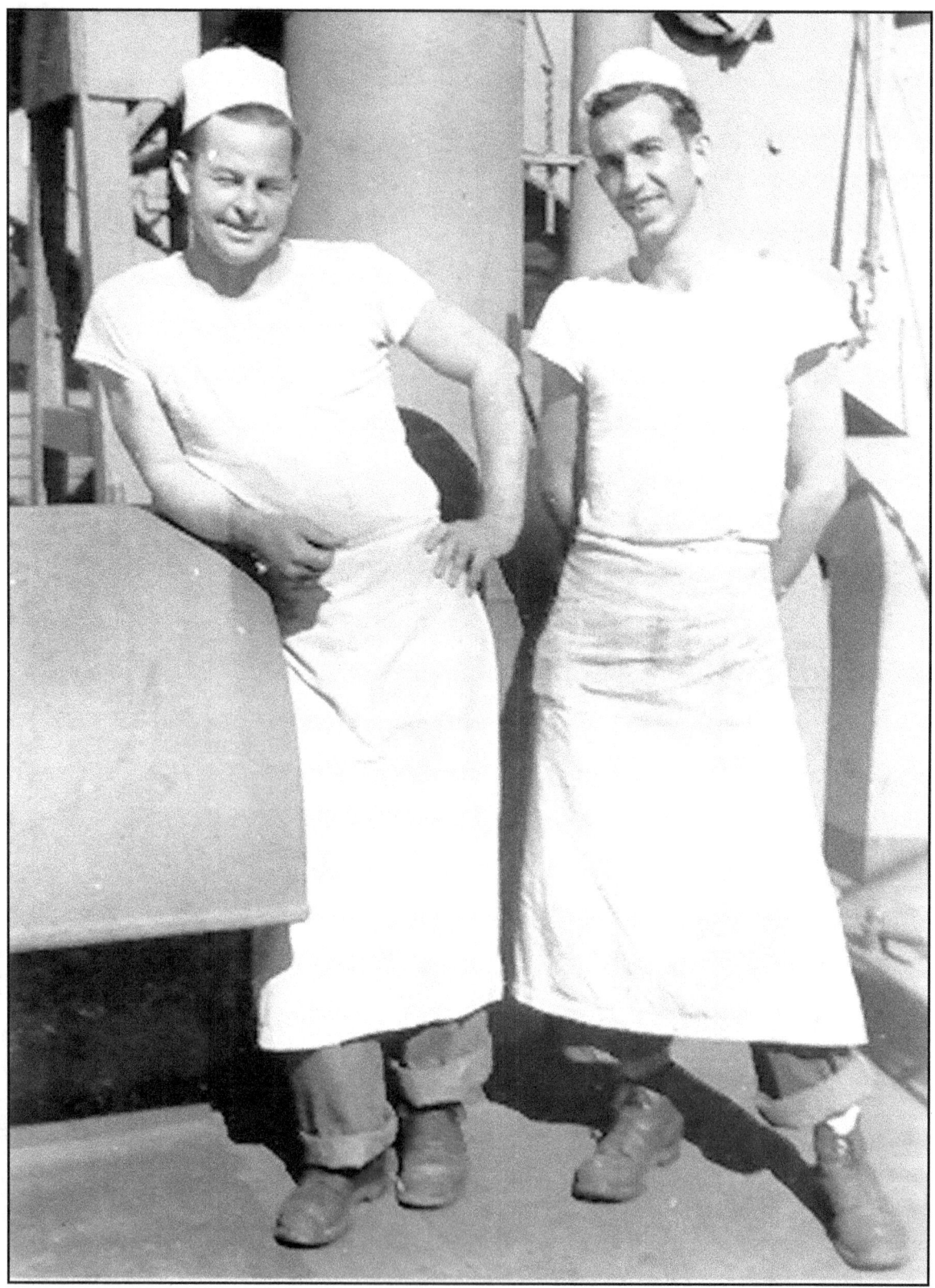

Chief William Provins (left) and cook "Little" Brown

Little Brown (Left) and Jack Denton on Leave in Honolulu

BLACK GANG IN BLUES - With Engineering Officer Robert D. Peter, ready for leave in Hawaii. Glen Oval 'Rosie' Rose is the tallest man from the left in the back row.

BLACK GANG IN WHITES - Glen Oval "Rosie" Rose at far upper left.

*From Left to Right, Top: Emery Stotts and J. C. Horner;
(Middle) LeRoy Parrick; (Bottom) Andrew Prokop and Jim Lipinski*

Boxers, Names Unknown

Leroy J. Parrick

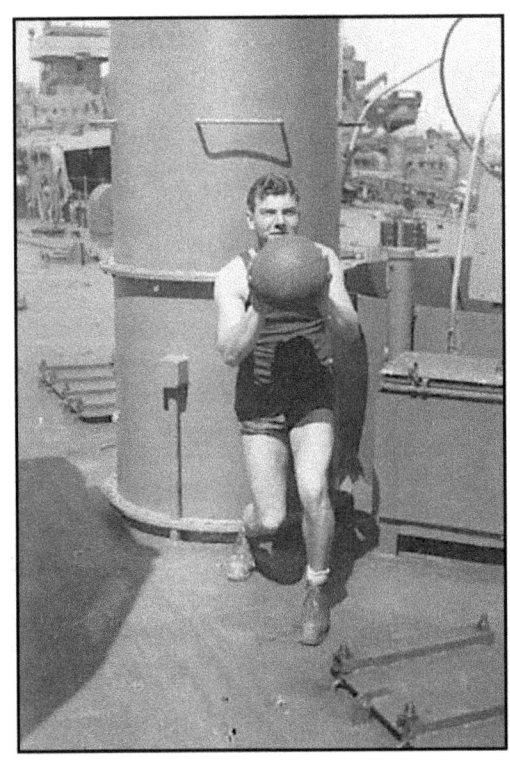

Glen O. Rose (left) and unknown crewmen. NOTE: Glen "Rosie" Rose was 6 foot and 6 inches tall, when bunks on the ship were only 6 feet long. He didn't get to stretch out very often!

*Crewmen Robert Christopher "Doc" Regel,
Arthur Joseph "Doc" Guida, and Joe Alexander "Doc" Terry*

Walter Bertouille (Left), Leanard Swazey and Roman Berzinski

Unnamed (Left), Elderidge Perry and Lillard Satterly

Engineering Officer Robert D. Peter Jr.

Unnamed crewman swabbing the deck

Robert Martin (at far right) and others unnamed, on liberty.

Carl Utberg on deck in blues, ready to go on liberty.

John Maher (left), John Walling (center), and Unknown at Portholes

Lee Wick

Hubert Orton Tinlin, D. L. Wever, Unnamed, and Charles G. Winters

Top: Jack Denton, Dave Ellis, and Earnest Abderhalden. Bottom: Leander "Lee" Wick, Joseph Paulik, and John B. Dismon

From Left to Right: H. E. Bullington, Dave Ellis, Frank Burns, and Leander Wick

Leander "Lee" Wick *Dave Ellis*

Cooks Dave Ellis (Left) and Frank Bunker

THE LADY LUCK

Lillard Satterly *Leanard Willis Swazey*

*Ship's battle record, painted on the Conning Tower
by Howard E "Buck" Bailey*

Chester "Goatie" Storegaard, Arthur Knutson, and D. L. Wever
December of 1945

Walter Bertouille (left) and unnamed crewmen on the deck

Gun Crew. (Top) - Leanard Swazey, James M. Ferrell, Frank Burns, Roman Berzinski, and Julius Swope; (Bottom) - Unnamed, Unnamed, Sal M. Magel (or Nagel), and Officer Gene Hanley

Sal Nagel (or Magel) loading and Leonard Swazey shooting

Thomas A. Page, on leave   *Nathaniel McCloud*

*Lillard Satterly, Mr. Hanley and Thurman Cox
Chipping Paint on Deck*

*Charlie O. Majors
working on deck*

*Henry Szersinski,
signing*

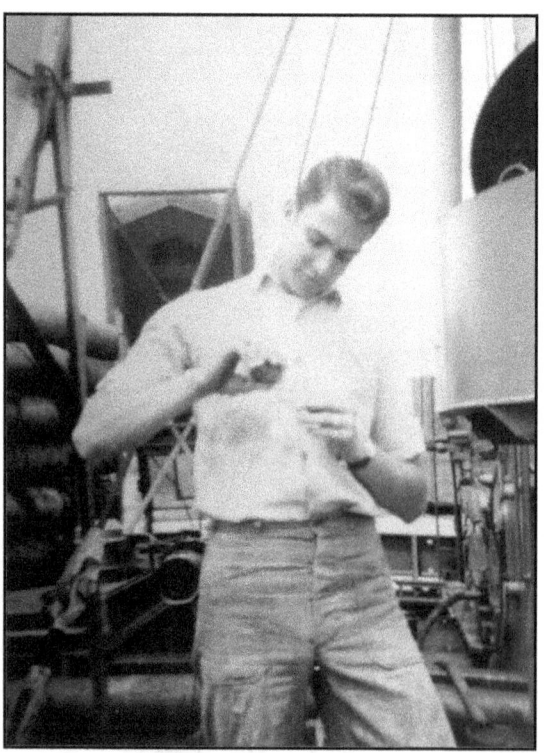

OFFICERS AND CREW OF THE USS LST-864

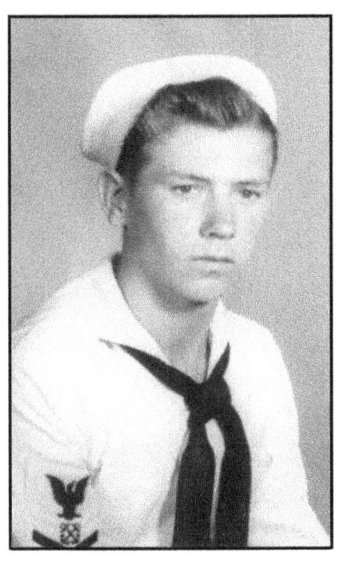

Ronald Miller   *Charles Francis Larkin*   *Gerald Langhett*

Leo "Curly" Leitl   *Charlie O. Majors*   *Name Unknown*

THE LADY LUCK

Tommy Thompson   *Herb Myers*   *Hugh Deyer*

J. W. Timpany   *Leonard Walczak*

OFFICERS AND CREW OF THE USS LST-864

Clinton Horner

Chester Storgaard

MOMM3c John Maher

Walter Bertouille, on Leave

Wilbur Brandmair   *William Reeble, Jr*

BUNK AREA OF LST-864
Jim Buckingham (left) and Andy DiPalma

Catholic Church service aboard ship in route to Okinawa.

WORK CREW ON DECK
Hugh Deyer, John Hammond, Unknown, Donald Emmel, and James Buckingham

Frank Burns (left), Robert Taylor (center), and Joe Dobesh

Unnamed officer and crewmen ashore at Mog Mog

Work crew on deck. From Left to Right: Unknown, Chief Rushing, Unknown, Frank Dobes, Unknown, and Unknown

Leroy Parrick (left) and Jim Buckingham, topside

CLOWNING AROUND ON DECK
TOP: Unnamed, Jim Lipinski, Roman Berzinski, and Howard "Buck" Bailey. BOTTOM: Johnny Ferraro, Leonard Swazey (wearing the wig), Frank Burns, and H. E. Bullington

Ronald Miller, Gerald Langhett, and Charles G. Winters

Crewmen at the open bay of the ship

Radiomen at work on deck, names unknown

*Tommy Thompson, James Holmes and
Joe Dobesh, working on deck*

LST-864 docked at Midway

CHAPTER 3

"THE LADY LUCK"

For the record, the United States Navy itself traces its ancestry to October 13, 1775, when an act of the Continental Congress authorized the first ship of a new navy for the *United Colonies*, as they were then known. By tradition, military ships were named in any number of ways until March 3, 1819, when an act of Congress formally placed the responsibility for assigning names to the Navy's ships in the hands of the Secretary of the Navy, a prerogative which he still exercises today.

The Secretary relies on many sources to help him reach his ship naming decisions. Each year, the Naval Historical Center compiles primary and alternate ship name recommendations and forwards these to the Chief of Naval Operations by way of the chain of command. These recommendations are the result of research into the history of the Navy and by suggestions submitted by service members, Navy veterans, and the public. As with many other things, however, the procedures and practices involved in Navy ship naming are as much, if not more, products of evolution and tradition as of legislation.

Ship name source records at the Navy Historical Center in Washington, D.C., reflect the wide variety of name sources that have been used in the past, particularly since World War I. Ship name recommendations are conditioned by such factors as the name categories for ship types that have been built, as approved by the Secretary of the Navy; the distribution of geographic names of ships of the Fleet; names borne by previous ships which distinguished themselves in service; names recommended by individuals and groups; and names of naval leaders, national figures, and deceased members of the Navy and Marine Corps who have been honored for heroism in war or for extraordinary achievement in peace.

After consideration at the various levels of command, the Chief of Naval Operations signs an annual memorandum recommending names for year's building program and sends it to the Secretary of the Navy. The Secretary considers these nominations, along with others he receives as well as his own thoughts in this matter. At appropriate times, he selects names for specific ships and announces them.

While there is no set time for assigning a name, it is customarily done before the ship is christened. The ship's sponsor--the person who will christen the ship--is also selected and invited by the Secretary. In the case of ships named for individuals, an effort is made to identify the eldest living direct female descendant of that individual to perform the role of ship's sponsor. For ships with other name sources, it is customary to honor the wives of senior naval officers or public officials.

Into the early years of the 20th century there was no fixed form for Navy ship prefixes. Ships were rather haphazardly identified, in correspondence or documents, by their naval type (U.S. Frigate ___), their rig (United States Barque ___), or their function (United States Flag-Ship ___). They might also identify themselves as "the Frigate ___," or, simply, "Ship ___." The term "United States Ship," abbreviated "USS," is seen as early as the late 1790s; it was in frequent, but far from exclusive, use by the last half of the 19th century.

On January 8, 1907, President Theodore Roosevelt issued Executive Order 549 to establish order and uniformity in the naming of naval vessels. The order directed that " . . . the official designation of vessels of war, and other vessels of the Navy of the United States, shall be the name of such vessel, preceded by the words, United States Ship, or the letters U.S.S., and by no other words or letters.

Today, the classification and status of naval ships and craft are defined in the United States Navy's Regulations of 1990, Article 0406. The Chief of Naval Operations remains responsible for the assignment of classification and names for administrative purposes to water-borne craft and the designation of status for each ship and service craft. Commissioned vessels and craft are identified by the words "United States Ship," abbreviated "U.S.S." Civilian manned ships, of the Military Sealift Command or other commands, designated "active status, in service" are identified by the words "United States Naval Ship," abbreviated "U.S.N.S." Ships and service craft designated "active status, in service," with some exceptions, are referred to by name, when assigned, classification, and hull number (e.g., "HIGH POINT PCH-1" or "YOGN-8").

World War I sparked an unprecedented level of naval ship construction, principally in destroyers and submarines, to protect the massive sealift effort--the "bridge of ships"--across the Atlantic to Europe. As World War II approached, and ship construction programs began to include new types of ships, these required new name sources; others required a modification of existing name sources to meet a perceived shortage of "appropriate" names.

Amphibious warfare, long considered a minor function by navies around the world, assumed major importance in World War II. It was this that led to the development of the entirely new "family" of ships, craft especially designed for massive landing operations in Europe and the Pacific. Many these new types of *"landing ships"* did not receive "word" names but were simply known by their hull numbers--*LST-806* and *LCI (G)-80*, for example.

Attack cargo ships and attack transports carried landing craft to put cargo and troops ashore on a beachhead. Many of these were named for American counties (*Alamance* [AKA 75]; *Hinsdale* [APA 120]). Some early APAs, converted from conventional troopships, kept their former names (*Leonard Wood, President Hayes*); many AKAs were named for stars (*Achernar*) or constellations (*Cepheus*). Dock landing ships, seagoing ships with a large well deck for landing craft or vehicles, bore names of historic sites (*Gunston Hall, Rushmore*). Modern LSDs are still part of today's Fleet, and carry on this name source (*Fort McHenry, Pearl Harbor*). After World War II the remaining tank landing ships (LST) were given names of American counties; thus, the previously unnamed *LST-819* now became *Hampshire County* (LST-819).

The prefix "USS," meaning "United States Ship," is used in official documents to identify a commissioned ship of the Navy. It applies to a ship while she is in commission. Before commissioning, or after decommissioning, she is referred to by name, with no prefix. Civilian-manned ships of the Military Sealift Command (MSC) are not commissioned ships; their status is "in service," rather than "in commission." They are, nonetheless, Navy ships in active national service, and the prefix "USNS" (United States Naval Ship) was adopted to identify them. Other Navy vessels classified as "in service" are simply identified by their name (if any) and hull number, with no prefix.

The LST-864 was one of many "Jeff-Works" assembly line ships manufactured under conditions of urgency during the early 1940s to assure an American victory in World War II. Many such "landing ships" were built, so many, in fact, that most of them were referred to their class name and number instead of by an individual ship name. It was, therefore, commissioned into service as the "USS LST-864," a "numbered" rather than a "named" ship.

It was dissatisfaction among the crew over serving on a numbered but unnamed vessel that brought "The Lady Luck" into existence. She was born when some of the crew decided to give their ship its own unofficial but personalized identity. According to crewman Jim Lipinski, her figure was drawn and then painted on the ship by crewman Byron Francis O'Brien, who had signed on out of Hartford, Connecticut. Both men were members of the ship's first crew. The two pages that follow show her as she originally drawn and, later on, as she appeared painted on the bow of the ship. Jim watched his shipmate Byron paint the good lady on the bow, and from that day forward the USS LST-864 was known as "The Lady Luck."

Drawing of The Lady Luck by LST-864 Crewman Byron Francis O'Brien

"Lady Luck" painted on the bow of the USS LST-864

SHIP'S BASKETBALL TEAM. LeRoy Parrick, Jr., Unknown, Unknown, Howard E. "Buck" Bailey, and Unknown

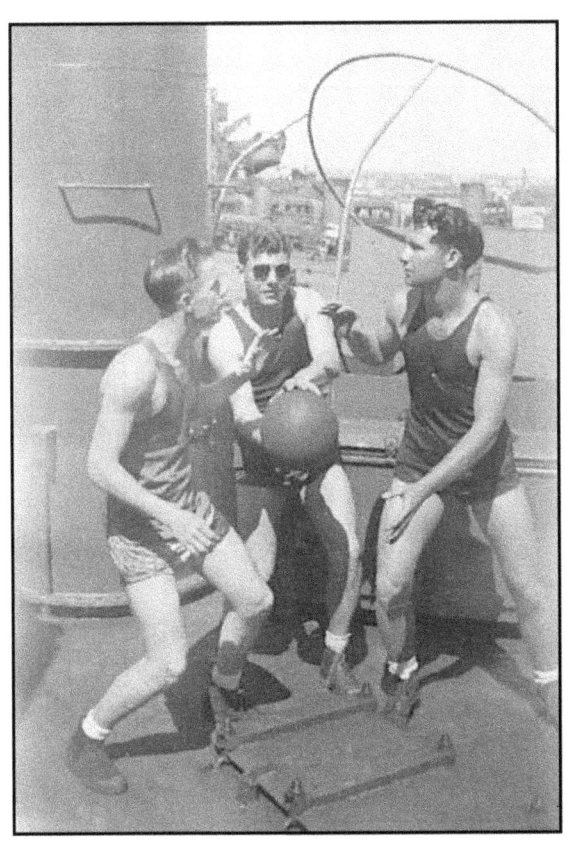 

Unnamed crewmen dressed in whites for leave

LST-864 headed for the Navy yard at San Francisco

CHAPTER 4

THE LADY LUCK AT WAR

Life at sea was a mix of many things--general quarters drills, hard work, tedium, loneliness, and fear. As part on an on-going effort to keep the men focused and sharp, the commanding officer of LST-864, Captain Richard B. Wathen, sent out occasional bulletins and memoranda to the men. The men received the following message from him on June 12, 1945:

---

*WARTIME MESSAGE
FROM THE CAPTAIN TO THE CREW*

On June 13th, this ship will have been in full commission six months. It is only natural that during such a period you, and myself as well, will get fed up with the monotony of our routine. However, in a six month period a steady routine followed through day after day will produce certain surprising results as the figures below indicate.

1. *Distance traveled - 19,450 nautical miles.*

2. *The tonnage of the three cargoes, plus pontoons and LCT we have carried multiplied by the mileage we have carried them gives a total of 11,133,000 ton miles!*

3. *The troops we have carried mulitiplied by the mileage we have carried them totals 2,160,000 troop miles.*

4. *By June 13th, the galley will have prepared 35,552 rations.*

5. *Assuming that we have no air attack before the 13th, we will have expended 18350 rounds of 20MM ammunition and 4,341 rounds of 40MM ammunition.*

6. By the 13th, Weaver and his Black gang will have succeeded in consuming about 228,000 gallons or diesel oil.

7. The bow anchor has been dropped and heaved in 38 times. The stern anchor 13 times.

8. The Medical Dept. so far has taken 40 sutures or stitches.

9. There have been 141 advancements in rating since commissioning.

10. The crew has aged approximately 55 years. Average age at commissioning was 21 years, six months. Average age now is 22.

11. We have been underway about 100 days and tied up or at anchor about 80 days.

There are certain other statistics that would be interesting but no figures have been submitted on them.

1. How many heads has Schuler leaned?

2. How many times has McCloud called Mitchell on the P.A.?

3. How many shirts have Chambless and Abderhalden washed?

4. What did Rushing and Harmon do the time they were away from the ship at Leyte?

So far we are not credited with shooting down any Jap planes and the Gunnery Officer's hopes of sailing into Tokyo Harbor have not materialized. However, we have performed every mission that has been assigned us. We have never taken on a combat load and then been forced to unload it because of engine trouble as the 862 did a month ago at Leyte. We have not had the misfortune of losing any lives in our routine work about the ship, i.e. the 863, one man killed falling down a hatch; the 821, one man killed lowering an LCVP.

We have suffered no damage beaching or retracting as the 960 did at Ie Shima. The 960 underwent 30 days repairs at Ulithi because of a damaged propeller and rudder. What I want to impress on the crew, is the fact that in this six months period we have produced certain very tangible contributions to the war effort.

I don't want you to lose sight of the importance of your work simply because it is a day in day out affair and you sometimes get fed up with what you are doing.

I mention the bad luck some other ships have had because I want you to realize that our job cannot be accomplished unless all hands are alert and do their part. There are two factors that have contributed to our record:

1.   Your good work and cooperation.

2.   The man we go to see on Sunday.

########

If factor number one is missing, number two will be also. The man we go to see on Sundays has a peculiar habit of giving most help to those people who make a. determined effort to HELP THEMSELVES.

The Commanding Officer,

Richard B. Walther

June 13, 1945

Lady Luck in a convoy of LSTs, heavily loaded with equipment and bound for the occupation of Japan after VJ Day. A movie screen is set up on deck.

Leanard Swazey and Frank Burns on Deck

Frank Bunker at a gun during a drill

Postcard depiction of a widely held sentiment aboard ship

Captain Wathen, supervising the loading of cargo

LST-864 deck-side view of landing on a beach at Ie Shima. Shows 40MM shelling of mountain peaks in distance

Newsman Ernie Pyle was killed near here, one morning in April of 1945

Unloading cargo on a beach at Ie Shima near Okinawa. Gun battery in foreground.

Trading films at sea with the USS LST-880 while in Convoy to Ie Shima and Okinawa in 1945

One mission accomplished; cargo bay emptied

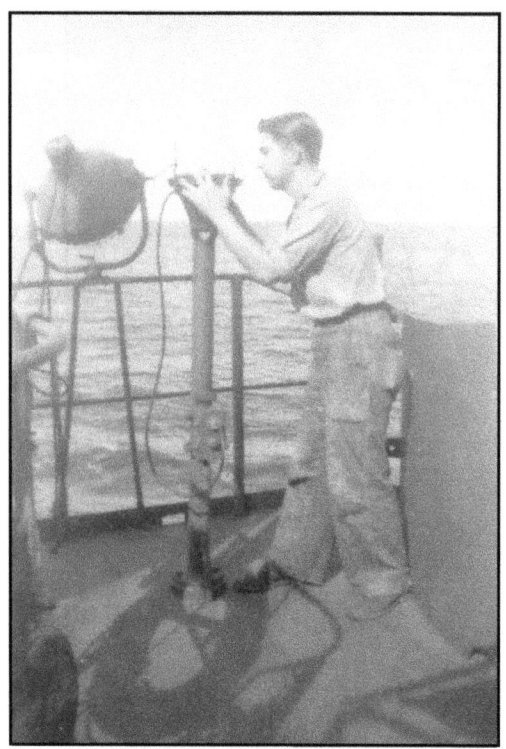

*QM2c Bill Mueller,
taking a bearing*

*Helmsman
QM2c Bill Mueller*

*GM2c Robert L. Gregg,
taking a reading*

*Work crew on deck,
names unknown*

Unnamed crewmen and Joe Dobesh unloading at Pearl Harbor

Loading LCT-831 at Pearl Harbor

Unloading LCT-1428, a tricky maneuver.

Crewmen loading in a small boat to go on liberty at Pearl Harbor

Dave Ellis (Left) and Lee Wick on leave at Pearl Harbor

Roman Berzinski (left) and LeRoy Parrick

Hula girl at Pearl Harbor

Berzinski, Burns, Swazey, Bertouille, Unknown, and Bullington

Malcolm Kaehler

H. E. Bullington

Unnamed Crewman

Robert L. Bell

Leonard Swazey

Unknown (Top Left), Jim Lipinski, Leonard Swazey (Bottom Left), and Unknown

H. E. Bullington (left), Frank Burns (Center), and Leonard Swazey

Hospital Ship USS Sanctuary berthed at Pearl in 1946, awaiting a trip to Japan

Leonard Swazey, signaling on the conning tower; other unnamed

Loading LST-864 at Pear Harbor for the trip to Japan

Frank Burns (left) and Joe Dobesh

Galley aboard the USS LST-864

Tug taken in San Diego Harbor in the Philippines

Chief William Robert Provins, on leave.

Beach Party in the Philippines

Outrigger canoe viewed off the ship

Soldier with a Filipino civilian

Filipino Peso saved as a souvenir during the war

Currency note issued by the Japanese government for use in the Philippines. Saved as a souvenir during the war.

*Filipino Woman
on the roadside*

*Unnamed, Unnamed,
and Dave Ellis on leave*

Filipino boys grinding meal

Crewmen on leave bought this fire engine and then drove it back to Frisco where they sold it for a profit. Merle Bauer (left) and Leanard Swazey

Prepared for Liberty. From left to right: Howard Bailey, Frank Burns, Roman Berzinski, Unnamed, H. E. Bullington and Unnamed

Provincial Capitol Building in Leyte, the Philippines

Crewmen ready to go on leave in the Philippines

Jail in Layte, the Philippines
"A poor place to spend a night."

Viewing a sunken Japanese ship. From L. to R.: Leonard Swazey, H. E. Bullington, Roman Berzinski, and Leonard Walczak

Radarmen: Unnamed (left), James Evans (center), and Unnamed

Sunken Japanese ship in Tokyo Bay

LST-864 unloading at Ie Shima

LST-864 unloading at Ie Shima.

Gun position near LST unloading site at Ie Shima.

Man-made dock for beach landing at Ie Shima.

LST-864 unloading at Yokosuka, Japan

Unloading LCT-831 off LST-864, a tricky operation.

Crewmen viewing the remains of a crashed Japanese plane at Ie Shima

Headed for liberty in a borrowed jeep

Ensign Gibson on leave at a shrine in Tokyo

Japanese Imperial Palace Grounds in Tokyo.

Japanese currency collected as a souvenir during the war. Front and back views at actual size.

Frank Burns (left) and J. W. Timpany departing on leave in Japan

Jack Denton on leave in Yokosuka, Japan

LST-864 docked in Japan. Pictured from left to right are Leanard Swazey, LeRoy Parrick, Frank Burns, Walter Bertouille, and H. E. Bullington

War damage observed by crewmen in leave in Japan

More war damage in Japan. Note the air raid tunnel in the street.

Nathaniel McCloud (left) and LST-864 Crewmen on leave in Yokosuka.

Jim Lipinski and J. W. Timpany in bombed out area of Yokosuka

Crewmen on leave in war damaged Yokosuka.

Crewmen on leave in Yokosuka. J. W. Timpany at left

J. W. Timpany
on leave in Yokosuka

Japanese girl
in Yokosuka

LST-864 crewmen Jim Lipinski, Andy DiPalma, and Frank Burns,
discussing international relations with Japanese girls in Yokosuka

Andy DiPalma (Left) and Jim Lipinski

Frank Burns with an unexploded bomb found at LST-864's Tokyo Bay landing site

Crewmen on liberty, talking with a guard at the Japanese Imperial Palace. From left to Right: Frank Burns, Merle Bauer, Roman Berzinski, and Jim Lipinski.

Japanese Serviceman

Japanese Navymen

Japanese Troops

Jim Lipinski talking with Japanese troops

Japanese kids on the streets of Yokosuka.

Merle Bauer at the railing aboard ship

Joseph Paulik

Japanese gun emplacement in a cave on Yokosuka

Japanese gun crew in surrender

Seaman Glen Rose on leave in Yokosuka

Crewman, negotiating a taxi fee in China, after the end of the war

Frank Burns, dancing with Miss China, after the end of the war

THE SCUTTLEBUTT

Life aboard ship could get lonely at times, and most crewmen took advantage of any means of communication available to them. Many cards and letters were sent to loved ones, and all crewmen eagerly anticipated the receipt of mail from home. Communication aboard ship was also aided by the "*Scuttlebutt,*" a newsletter published by members of the crew. Because it provided a welcome diversion from daily routine, new editions were looked forward to by officers and crewmen alike. It was also an item that could be mailed home to anxious family members. Several issues of the Scuttlebutt appear in the pages that follow.

Mother's Day card sent home during the war by crewman John Paul "Pops" Gainor

A mail ship, making a delivery at sea.

Exchanging films at sea with LST-1081

LADY LUCK'S SCUTTLEBUTT

New revised edition of the ship's paper formerly known as the "Lollypop".

Semi-Annual publication of our weekly edition. Weather: Ask Mr. Haines, he's infallible.

Published June 19, 1945 at sea by and for the men of the U.S.S. L.S.T. 864 — Vol I, Exition I

LADY LUCK' BACK FROM OKINAWA FOR SECOND TIME — TOJO PERTURBED

RECAPITULATION OF THE SITUATION:-

February 25, 1945, that fateful day when the shores of the U.S.A. faded into the background and ahead lay - who knew what. Twenty five hundred miles of green Pacific stretched before us, twelve days underway, monotonous routine and then---Hawaii---the land of pineapples, grass skirts, and what have you. It was a beautiful morning, March 7th, when Diamond Head, the highest peak on Oahu loomed into view, and the U.S.S. L.S.T. 864 put into Hawaii.

It was all work and very little play at Pearl, with all hands busy preparing for what lay ahead. Five days later we bid "Aloha" to the last outpost of American life and headed out to new horizons. Twelve days later found us in Eniwetok, Marshall Islands a small atoll wrested from the Japs about a year ago. We spent but a few hours at this outpost, time enough to pick up our welcome mail, and then on to Guam.

Three days later found us at this base and a well supplied activity it is. We spent three days at Guam replenishing our supplies and a quick look at Guam proved very interesting. Many remains of the enemy's control of the Island are still present, & it was our first opportunity to view such things - but not our last.

Our ship then pushed on to our last stop before our first encounter with the Jap... Ulithi, in the Caroline Islands, about 900 miles south-west of Guam. We were at this quite pleasant outpost for ten days and aside from replenishing our stock, all hands took full interest in the various recreational opportunities offered.......namely Mog Mog Island and Beer.

On April 12th, we bid adieu to Ulithi and headed our bow Northward toward Okinawa Shima and IE Shima in the Ryukyu Islands, 350 miles from the Japanese homeland. After 11 days of varied and diverting entertainment, we steamed southward again to Ulithi and from Ulithi the next stop was Leyte in the Philippines and then back to our old stamping grounds, Okinawa Shima.

This is the second time we've headed away from that Jap infested hell-hole, having discharged two cargoes. Now slant-eyed Tojo need not be too optimistic......we'll be right back with more.

Box Score: Japs, minus one Island and 40000 fleas.
L.S.T. 864: Plus two stars in her Asiatic Pacific Campaign Ribbon.

OKINAWA SHIMA; land of grass huts, fleas and miniature, buck-toothed tiny tims; a winter resort for the Japanese looking more like a last resort, as the LST 864 sailed the China Sea, one bright April morning.

Since then, the general attitude of the crew has improved greatly. At last we feel that we are in the fight and no longer just another LST waiting around for someplace to go.

We've experienced air-raids and learned that our guns could fire at something besides a red sleeve. We've all learned how the crew as a whole would react under fire, and last but not least, just exactly who the enemy is and for what he stands.

Most of the Japanese we've seen could be termed "Good" Japanese being that they were either sprawled out face down or in POW camps. However they are the enemy and their might is nothing to be sneezed at. We must all devote ourselves to our respective jobs so that we can do them better than ever. By doing this, we too can hope to achieve the same victory our ship-mates have achieved in Europe.

ROTATION FOR L.S.T. SAILORS.

To most of the fellows aboard ship, the rotation plan is just another miserable joke of the war. We have listed below the qualifications for return to the states, as compiled by men on duty in the Pacific:

(1) Applicant must have at least 44 years continuous sea duty.
(2) He must have lost an arm or leg receiving also at least five of the following citations: Purple Heart, Silver Star, Medal of Honor, DSC, Legion of Merit or Bronze Star.
(3) Applicants must be physically fit—free from ring worm, athlete's foot, jungle rot, colds, coughs, malaria, or typhus fever.

- continued on page 2

Scuttlebutt of June 19, 1945, page 1

STATION PLAN - continued from page one.

(4) If having lost an arm, applicant must be able to write his name with the nub of his elbow to prove his usefulness in the states.
(5) Any man who dies while waiting for approval to his application, will be considered as having rejected stateside duty and therefore be buried overseas.

- - - - - - - - - - - - - - - -

WAR IN LOUISVILLE
(Chapter one)

There we were, in no man's land at 0645 one cold bleak November morning. To our right stood a broken down shack (residents called it a station), to our left, miles of jungle and stone. Atop the one room smoky shack was wired a sign creaking in the cold Indiana wind. "Jeffersonville, Indiana".

Most of the men sitting on the "Grand Central Station" of Jeff were wondering where the town was. I was wondering where the State was.

Being a New Yorker and critic of all states and cities, I decided I'd be the advanced guard and ride the baggage truck, to this day, I have yet to see Jeff. We stopped at a street light, but I don't believe that was the town. Although my brother said it was. Perhaps I was looking in the other direction. I must make it a point to check on that after the war.

After a ride of about 10 minutes, we arrived at Jeff Boat and Machine Co., the administration building deeply impressed me, the women looking out the windows did more than impress me. But being an Officer, I felt it my duty to let the enlisted men enjoy the fruits of this campaign. An Officer must set example.

Within ten minutes our men had dates for the next month. I supervised the complete operation.

Eventually we weighed anchor and set sail for Louisville, Ky, and through clouds of dense smoke I saw green Ky, from the famous bridge often called the "Gateway to the South". We set the special sea detail, and dropped the hook at the YMCA. Our men quickly set up headquarters in the YMCA, and I set sail for the "Brown". About an hour later, I got the word that our men are abandoning the "Y", seems their liberty was being defied, and our men being bold and independent, were leaving by every available exit....windows, stairs, ropes, etc......
Even the manager was impressed when he was told where he could go. When the elevator secured to Navy Personnel, gear went out windows. It was the first test of our crew's resourcefulness. It showed their character.

By evening, the crew is set up in the best and worst hotels in Louisville. Were squared away clicking like a clock. All we have to do is round them all up in the morning in front of the "Y" and drive out to Jeff----(to be continued in next issue)..

"COULD YOU BE A SAILORS WIFE"

Can you sit home nights until the war is won?
Can you offer him forgivness for everything he has done?
Can you stand the penny pinching you are forced to do?
Can you watch them in their new clothes and let you old one pull you thru?
Can you make a meal special, and cook it eighteen different ways?
And use the nights to keep house and work thru-out the days?
Can you stand the months of waiting until his sweet returns?
Can you stretch a hundred dollars from the seventy-eight he earns?
Can you darn his worn out stockings, and patch and sew and mend?
Can you save some extra money, that he doesn't even send?
Can you wear a dress for Sunday, and wear it every day?
Can you stand civilian gossip, and everything they say?
Can you admire others jewelry, and have none of your own?
And watch others eating beefsteak, while you chew a meatless bone?
Can you do your own hair waving, and beauty treat yourself?
Can you get along with nothing, and put all desires on the shelf?
Can you stop and make coffee a dozen times a day?
Can you always say your ready, when he thinks he wants to play?
Can you write a daily letter and fill it full of love?
Make him think he's just your ideal, a gift from God above?
Can you smile through tears and heartaches and trust him all your life?
If you can, you are recommended to be a SAILORS WIFE...........

- - - - - - - - - - - - - - - -

Did you know.........
That the LST 864 was in the newsreels up on the beach at IE Shima?
That we have travelled over 19,900 miles?
That the galley has prepared over 35,600 rations?
That we have expended 18,350 rounds of 20MM ammunition and 4,341 rounds of 40MM ammunition?
That we have consumed over 228,500 gallons of diesel oil?
The medical department has taken 40 sutures or stitches.
That "POP" Gainor is the oldest man in the crew (being 38) and Adair is the youngest (17 years old)?
That we haven't had fresh milk in 4 months
That "Tippy" has learned to shake hands?
"Tyrone" DiPalma gets more mail than any other person on the ship?
That Stotts is beating Truesdale in the "Sacking-In" contest?

///////// NUFF SAID /////////////////

This page may be torn out if you desire...

BREAKFAST AT SARDI'S
by the Original American Indian or commonly known as Black Mac.

As the sun comes out of the eastern sky, the tastey aroma of half cooked bacon and cold powdered eggs floats noiselessly thruout the passageways of the good ship "lollypop"; Mitchell stirs restlessly in his sack. At precisely 0645, the messenger starts his round-robin trips to wake the Steward-Mates, succeeds in doubtful. Finally the excitement is too much and THERE OFF: "and it's "BIRD CRAP" on the rail, with "BIG BALL" riding low to the ground and "PECKER" running for all he's worth. And there goes "PREGNANT LADY" out in front at the three quarter turn. Coming around the turn it's "RUBBER" in the stretch with "HORSE STUFF" dropping to the rear. And coming into the finish line it's "BIG DICK" who wins by a head." The table is set; the food is out and the Officers are now being awakened by Mitchell and McCloud. The first man out is always the Chief Engineer with Simon the Slaver not far behind; not a word is spoken. "Now, I've got an uncle", commences the Chief only to be interrupted by the noisy entrance of Clyde Beatty and his trained animal who figures that all meals should be run on a communistic basis and he wants his share - Clyde encourages this which always adds to the confusion. Then in comes "Grewsome"; you never see the gruesome twosome together at breakfast - one or the other can always be found in the sack. This morning, as is generally the case, Jake is the absent member. Everybody always asks, "Where is Jake?" As if they didn't know! In comes "El Gringo" with his red hair all messed up; it's then that "Grewsome" and his cronies of the galley take a beating. "Gringo" always gets more pleasure out of shoving his plate away in front of "Grewsome" than he does in appeasing his overly developed hunger. Hell breaks loose when the "Tigre" comes in; he always gets there just in time to be late for breakfast yet early enough to argue the point; and he does. It generally ends up that the galley has to restart the ovens and do breakfast all over again. When his plate is finally ready, Mitchell trips into the Wardroom with joy in his heart and lead in his ...., but I've seen the time when he could hurry. The "Tiger" then delights in saying, "This breakfast isn't fit to eat; I'll just take a cup of coffee". There's not much the wild men from Borneo can do, so they go ahead and clear off the table. "Well boys", says the "Tiger", "bet I can get more extra men tonight for extra duty than any two of you put together." And so the bets start. Simon the Slaver and Tiger running a close race. "All bets ....

– continued in next column....

have to be closed by 0900 .... says "Grewsome" "I've got to get my .... "Why doesn't somebody wake up "Jake", sayd somebody..."What could he do after he got up anyway?" says another. "Will let him sleep then; he's harmless." "Where is pudgey?", "Oh, he's on the conn. War's HELL says "Grewsome"; "I'm going back to bed".

Now you boys working in the galley, keep up the good work after all they're just Ensigns. An Ensign, you know, is a boy scout getting Chief's pay. Wait till they make (j.g.) then you can worry.

"I've got a bottle of Champagne, baby; Mebbe we can launch a boat or something"

PREGNANT IDEAS
The big stork; he brings the big healthy babys.......
The middle-sized stork, he brings the the average sized babys...........
And the little stork....well, he just scares the hell out of high school girls.

AOL
A sailor returned AOL from his week-end liberty using as his only excuse that when he arrived home, he found his wife taking a bath.
"But" questioned his Captain, "how does that explain your being AO.?"
"Well Sir", explained the sailor, "It took some time for my clothes to dry".

Little fly upon the wall........
Ain't you got no folks at all....
YOU BASTARD!

Do you want to hear the joke about the Olives?...........See Bell.

Scuttlebutt of June 19, 1945, page 3

"LADY LUCK'S SCUTTLEBUTT"
Official Publication Of The
U.S.S. L.S.T. 864, %·F.P.O., San Fran.
EDITOR: "Doc" Guida, PhM1c
CO EDITOR: Bob Bell, Y2c
CARTOON by: Frank Bunker.

The editor gratefully acknowledge receipt of the articles contributed by the Officers and Men.

FAREWELL TO A SHIPMATE

Recently at Okinawa, the crew experienced the loss of a fellow friend and shipmate, Ernest A. Fry. Fry was transferred to a hospital ship because of an injury incurred during an air raid at Okinawa. Unlike the other shipmates we have lost, Fry had been with us since the crew was formed and he helped make it what it is today. To Ernie, the entire crew of Officers and Men bid a "Get well soon" and "Good Luck Always".

A COUPLA JOKES..

"All men not going up for rates can laugh at this:"

Cutie: "I'm going to marry an Officer and a gentleman."
Sailor: "But honey, that would be bigamy".

\# \# \# \# \# \# \#

Farmer's Wife: "Is this the druggist speaking?".
Druggist: "Yes Mam".
Farmer's Wife: "Well, be sure and write plain on them bottles which is for the horse and which is for my husband. I don't want nothing to happen to that horse before Spring plowing."

SPEND YOUR MONEY THE EASY WAY !

Shop in comfort at ISAAC'S Bargain Basement, only two floors down. Take advantage of our assorted stock and when you come in, "Don't say how much, say how many".

Ed Note: This is a paid add..paid in blood.

SPORT HI-LITES

During the past few months, the crew's basket-ball team has had the opportunity to show it's stuff against teams of various fleet units. At Ulithi, and then again at Leyte, the team met all types of opposition and displayed a great amount of sportsmanship and skill. Previously the enlisted men's team had been playing the Officers, but at Leyte, arrangements were made by which they could get a crack at some other teams.

cont. on next column

The first few games seemed to get away from the boys, but those few defeats only strenghthened them for the bigger games to come. The LST 862 continued to be a problem having been the victor in two successive games. However, the 864 remedied this when they originated a team comprised of the stars of the crew. This all-star team consisted of Ensign Haines, Ensign Holland, and Ensign Holmes together with two enlisted men Horner and Lipinski.

The 862 fell twice before the deadeye scoring of the "ferocious five"; To date they have beaten all opposition, including the Leyte Harbor champs. But this is only the beginning; there are many more games to play and they will win them too with the entire crew to cheer them on.

GUNNER'S MATES, MAKE SMOKE.

When this familiar command is passed over the PA, out of their mussed-up sacks with sleep-squinted eyes the gunner's mates crawl. The "Chief" Gunner's mate, John Phillip Ferraro, as his friends call him, will always be found brushing his way past crap games and around poker games until at last he reaches his destination, that beat-up twice exploded smoke generator on the fantail. Immediately he is joined by his colleague in crime, Julius H. Swope, GM2c and together the two of them fiendishly concoct the smoke-burping brew.

Eventually the smoke begins to penetrate the compartments of the ship. As it reaches the messing compartments, Isaac Newton Pitts has been seen to leave his pesos and centavos and even a straight flush in his mad scramble to the ship's service compartment to make sure it's not his fifteen cent cigars that are burning. Both bakers Joe Paulik and Jack Denton hasten to their ovens to assure themselves that their bakeries haven't caught fire. Incidently those two rookie bakers have been doing a swell job, filling in the shoes of Charlie Brown.

Finally the order for them to stop making smoke is passed and they venture forth to quiet their "Belching Betsy". After several polite, pleading, PA announcements the smoke clears and the gunner's mates tumble wearily into their now cold sacks. But don't go to sleep now boys, not yet, in a little while you'll have to go thru it again and so the vicious cycle continues............

IT ALL COMES OUT IN THE WASH....OH YEH!

The ship's laundry is the place on the tank deck where a big wheel eats hell out of your skivvies and a guy sits in front it reading a magazine. Chambless and Abd halden boast the fact that they operate only laundry where when the laundryman insults the customer, the customer doesn't threaten to discontinue his business there but threatens to increase it.

Scuttlebutt of June 19, 1945, page 4

LADY LUCK'S SCUTTLEBUTT

Our monthly Edition of our weekly paper published at Yokuska Japan.

WEATHER: Warmer; will be cooler when we hit the states.

Published October 5th, 1945 at sea by and for the men of the USS LST 864 Vol. I No. 3

"LADY" IN FIRST OCCUPA-TIONAL FORCE ENTERING JAPAN PROPER

ON THE SERIOUS SIDE

We all like to feel that with the passage of the years we are somehow & in some way becoming better and wiser. This does not necessarily mean that we are more skilled with our hands, or that we are quicker mentally and can add a sum of figures in less time than we could a year ago. It is good to know that our manual and intellectual ability is improving from day to day but essentially, that is not what we mean by becoming better and wiser.

What we do mean is that as time goes on we are becoming adjusted to life and the problems of life; that we feel more at ease about things in general. This is the wisdom that we like to think comes with the passage of time.

One of the keys to achieving this adjustment to living is <u>tolerance for our fellow man</u>. During our time in the service we have had a chance to learn more about tolerance than probably at any other period in our lives.

Whether on this ship, or on others we have seen every cross section of America taking the same chances that we take, living the way we live, and all doing a job that has helped bring Victory and Peace. Rich and poor, white and black, Jew and Gentile, have all made their contribution, and are worthy of our respect. The memory of this combined achievement of our people is something we should carry with us for the rest of our lives. In the future, whether we are striker in a picket line, or a prosperous business man;

(cont. on page four)

Yokosuka Japan, Tokyo Bay: LLSMB 0900:

As we left the placid beaches of Saipan enroute to Pearl Harbor Hawaii, the Island of beautiful hula-hula girls gracefully swaying to the strings of Hawaiian guitars on the moonlit beach of Waikiki, a strong rumor was circulating throughout the ship that this time we were headed for the States. Upon arrival at Pearl, we found out that we were to take a combat load of Communications Men in on the invasion of Japan. Our hopes of the states broken, we then turned to the peaceful beaches and recreation resorts of Hawaii for comfort. As we walk down the broad street of Nimitz Blv'd, we see for miles and miles sailors and more sailor Aha! theres a girl, no, it was just an illusion. Well, we might try and find a bar and sip a few cold beers. As we stand in line for two hours or more we suddenly find out that there is no beer to be had in Hawaii, only Rum and Cokes and they are rationed one to a person. Let's give up, we can at least hear records back on the ship.

Our combat load aboard and ready to shove off, it was then that the news arrived; the news that everyone had waited so long for, the war was over. Ship's whistles blew, bells rang, fog horns sounded and everyone in Hawaii began celebrating V-J day. A few days later, we shoved off for Midway Island, enroute Japan. The "Lady Luck" was the first LST to arrive at Midway since the war with Japan started. After a brief stay of about 4 or 5 hours, we proceeded on our way and arrived in Tokyo Bay to be greeted by our 3rd and 5th Fleets which made one of the greatest Naval gatherings in History. We unloaded our troops at Yokosuka's large Naval Base, and the majority of the crew made a tour of the base soviener hunting and getting a look at Jap equipment. Liberty in Yokosuka began that afternoon. The Japanese people were running about, some abandoning their caves and holes in the mountains and coming back to their homes and others starting their business establishments anew.

cont. on next p.

Scuttlebutt of October 5, 1945, page 1

THE LADY LUCK

SPORTS IN GENERAL....

Sports aboard this ship have been confined lately to such things as card playing, checkers, shooting the breeze and of course not to leave out that strenous game of "Hitting the sack" which everyone seems to enjoy the most, but now that all decks are cleared once again it won't be long now. (I can smell that oil of wintergreen already).

When we first arrived here at Japan, it was noticed that some of our allies (Marines and such) had already set a ball field on Green Beach and by some trick of fate we were beached there the next day to unload. Naturally, they couldn't resist that challange to the "Gyrenes". I would like to report that our boys wiped the field with them but sad to say such was not the case, in other words, we took an artistic shellacing. The fellows came back to the ship smarting under that defeat and just couldn't believe it had happened...sooooo....back again the next day for some more. This time a double header, no less. Never let it be said that an "Amphibian" gives up. Those "leathernecks" sure are lucky that we had to move out, eh fellas?....Yea. Its getting a little late for base ball any how.

Out basket ball team still looks good although Mr. Holland will be missed. We all think that Mr. Haines, Mr. Holmes, Campbell, Lipinski, Horner and a few others are good enough to take on any team around here. Throw in "Abe" Mueller, QM2c as the time keeper and how can we miss. The court suffered none the worst for wear and will soon be ready for the works. Intra-Division league has been going very well even though the Third Divisions "TIRD-BIRDS" have been running away with it up to now. The rest of the teams are more than determined to stop their undefeated streak. The lowly "HE-MEN" regret the loss of their key man Bauer, Y3c and Guida, PhM1c but promise a much stronger team with new additions such as Horner, S1c and Knapp, FC2c, Doug Campbell S1c, and the manager "Hatchy" Regel, PhM1c. "Hatchy" has pulled a few strings. We are waiting to see the reaction of the "DECK-APES" on this fast one. (Take that knife out of my back). Don't be surprised to see "TIPPIE" on Regels team one of these day's. That guy is capable of most anything.

Boxing doesn't seem to be taking up anybodys time except perhaps "Canvas-Back" Harry Szerzinski, "Sachel-Foot" Lipinski, "One-punch" Evans, "Leffty" Stotts "Light, Light, Light Heavyweight" Bunker and a few others. The trouble seems to be that the boys are tired of punching each other around and cant erest other ships to compete against them. might be just as well at that.

cont in next column

OCCUPATION OF JAPAN (cont)

The majority of the crew visited Yokohama and Tokyo and were able to admire the work that our B-29's and other aircraft had accomplish. Block after Block of buildings were complete demolished and there were very few buildings throughout the city that were left standing. The Japanese people were very friendly and polite and would salute or bow as an American sailor or soldier would pass by. While we were anchored in the bay, some of the crew salvaged a Jap Patrol Boat and were running it around the Harbor. They also converted a large charcoal burning truck into a gasoline burner and we now have an official liberty bus. After two weeks in Japan, we then set sail for Leyte, in the Philippine Islands, the same bay we were in once before, and once again the scuttlebutt started "is it the sta this time"?

* * * * (cont) from last column.

We now have a new sport, the game that has made all that strenous training that we all went through back at Bradford worthwhile A game which requires great coordination between the mind and the muscle and especially stamina. We refer to that Greatest of all sports "Monoply". (Man have I been out here too long). The local champion seems to be Utberg, SM3c. He must have been born in Palistine, he sure is a wizard with a buck. How about a monoply league for the old men that can't keep up with the younger fellows. It should prove to be a god send to those bench warmers like Pitts, SK2c; Thomas, EM2c, Mullen, EM2c, Nagel, GM3c, O'Brien, CM2c (what am I saying) that all, brother, thats all..........

* * * * * * * * * *

WELCOME!

Just as men are transferred from our ship men are received aboard to carry on the nam of the famed Lady Luck. CM2c Joe Timpany no shares the ship-fitters shop and PhM3c Lee Wooster is now 3rd Medical Advisor. FC2c Bob Knapp now shares a place in the Gunnery Division and S1c Doug Campbell is doing ver well behind a desk in the personnel office. S1c "Stoker" Carlton (Feed-em-their-hungry) is received in the humble presence of the "Deck-Apes". Good luck to each and every one of you.

* * * * * * * * * *

NOTICE ALL BEER GUZZLERS

Ship's Service will sponser a beer party just as soon as we reach Leyte and get our supplies set up. All the beer you can drink. Come one, come all. Also, a tour of the Philippine Island will be taken on our new liberty bus, the "Sad-Suky".

PAGE TWO

Scuttlebutt of October 5, 1945, page 2

AWARDS

The men in the crew are now authorized to wear the American Theater Ribbon; the Asiatic Pacific Ribbon with two (2) bronze stars; the Philippine Liberation Ribbon and just as soon as an AlNav comes out, will be entitled to the Japanese Occupational and Victory Ribbon.

* * * * * * * * * *

POINTS

The new Navy point system; the current topic of conversation throughout the ship these last few weeks, and why not? Doesn't 44 points allow us to put on the gray gaberdiens with a blue and yellow tie? Doesn't 44 points allow us to go out to the movies or go dancing without filling out a liberty chit? The system has been changed in the past week, they now include sea duty, and that gives most of us 2½ more points to add to our previous points. The way the new letter on the point system states, they will lower the points just as soon as possible, so, at least some of us will get to go home soon. There are a few men on board that the point system doesn't mean much to, for example Isaac Pitts, who's trying to ship over for 20 years and "Hashmark" Mullen, the man that says "Seven Hashmarks or I'll die trying". Good for you Mullen, your the kind of man this Navy needs.

* * * * * * * * * * * * * * * * * *

Now, just as soon as they open the doors, you stick your foot inside!

NIGHT LIFE IN LOUISVILLE

Liberty in Louisville was ideal. People loved sailors and the sailors loved people. What more could a Navy man want. Wherever he went, he was greeted with open arms. A heaven compared to Norfolk, where sailors and dogs were warned to keep off the grass.

The "Blue Grass Room" of the Hotel Brown was perhaps the most reserved and idealistic spot in town. The atmosphere was typically southern and definately Kentucky. Beautiful dance floor, mirrored overheads and a touch of New York in the drinks. Dreamy, sweet & soft music will always bring one back to those fast, short hours spent amony very pleasant company at the Blue Grass Room.

Around the corner and down a square or two (as Emmel would say), is the Henry Clay Hoetl. What makes the Henry (cont on next column)

LOUISVILLE (cont)

Clay famous? Why, it's the Chystal Terrace.

Nightly our crew would muster on the quarter deck of the Chrystal Terrace and decide what to do. With a drink in one arm and a girl in the other arm, they would decide the fate of the evening. Let me make it known that married men in the crew never showed up here. (Thomas, you can pay me tomorrow for that plug). After an hour or two of drinks, time was getting heavy, (so were the girls and the smoke), besides the medows always look greener on the other side and the men of the "Lady" beat a hasty retreat to the "Muscians Club". Twas at this club our men tasted action and saw blood. (Some of it belonged to them). Seems a man twisted a girls arm and the girl, being very demure and sweet hit him softly over the head with a bottle (full too). The manager trying to restore peace and order stepped out on the floor and a sailor, one of our beloved Ferry Crew boys, gave him his 14 point plan consisting of a lable & necessary accessories right on his nose. That, dear readers, was the straw that broke the camels back. From there on in, it was kill or be killed. Shrapnel was heavy and tables became air raid shelters. Women screamed and bottles flew. When the emergency air raid shelters became ammunition, our crew decided to leave via the back entrance. (cont. on next page)

PAGE THREE

Scuttlebutt of October 5, 1945, page 3

LOUISVILLE (cont)

Clothes, hats and drinks were left for the authorities who were streaming through all available doors. Night life in Louisville sure was wonderful. Seldom were nights spent as above. Usually it was a quiet evening in a quiet bar or dance hall or some other social function. The memories of pleasant hours spent in a very fine town will never fade in the minds of our nucleus crew. The city was given to us and everything in it was ours. To sailors, hungary for a liberty town where one was treated as a human being, Louisville was and is one of the greatest cities in America. What it lacks in size, it makes up in friendleness. Never once did a sailor hear a remark "run them down, their only sailors", it was always "Come in sailor, what can I do for you."

* * * * * * * * * * * * * * * * *

BON VOYAGE!

In Pearl Harbor and Yokosuka, 14 men of our crew were transferred either to other ships or back to the good old Uncle Sugar. Ensign Jack Holland, first Lieutenant or our ship returned to the states on an emergency leave and CCS Art Harmon, our poker ace, was transferred to the Demolition Combat Team at Pearl for duty. Among the men who were transferred to Base Hospitals or Hospital Ships were S1c Johnny Dismon; Cox Bill Reeble; and S1c Joe (Gizmo) Zorich. The men who were sent back to the States for leave and rehabilitation were: SK3c Harry (jack-of-the-dust) Jensen; GM1c Johhn (the lady killer) Ferraro; Bkr2c Charlie Brown; SC2c Guille Brown; SC3c Bob Martin. MoMM2c H.O.Tinlin received the sad news of his Mothers death and returned home immediately, on an emergency leave. Two of the luckiest guys on the ship that returned to the U.S. were MoMM2c Charlie Larkin, and S1c Jess Marshall who were sent back for discharge. While at Pearl Harbor, we were ordered to transfer one of our best friends; Y3c Merle Bauer who has been with us since commissioning. He was stationed at Pearl as a personnel yeoman. Lets hope that this time, we will all be able to go back together.

* * * * * * * * * * * * * * * * *

DON'T FORGET!!!

Shop at Isaac's Bargain basement for polite service; cut-rate prices and quick service. "Don't say how much, say how many!" Stop in anytime between the hours of 1800 and 1830.

864 IN THE ETHER

A radio program initiated by Mr. Holmes and Ship's Control Division began operation while at Yokosuka. All ships in Yokosuka Ko benefited by the program which was named, station "JERK". Many ships requested tunes and station J.E.R.K. was grateful to acknowledge them. Mr. Holmes did a swell job as MC, just another Fred MacMurray. Our crew had their own requests which might be called the Hit Parade of 64. "Forget-Me Nots in your eyes" was the favorite of all and especially Mr. Wood. Swope GM2c selected "In the Mood" by Glenn Miller, while Bob Bell Y2c picked "Guess I'll hang my tear out to dry" by Harry James. Mitchell, Ck3c played "Bear Cat Crawl" every time he was alone in the "studio". You could see Emmel get that far away look in his eye when they played "Til we meet again". The theme song "Let's Dance" by B.G. is a favorite of all. Naturally Walzak's favorite was "Louise" and who couldn't guess why. Jess Sowder and Pugs Satterly's favorite is "When my Blue Moon turns to Gold again". Bullington' favorite song, although it hasn't been written yet is: "Dear John". Bertouille and Rushing cuddle up when "Nancy" is played. Yes, even boys swoon over Sinatra when he sings a song like that. Jack Neal's favorite is "My Blue Heaven" by Glenn Miller and his Army Air Corps band. Upon arrival at Leyte, we hope to start up our half hour program nightely, so, tune in on station J.E.R.K. at 1800 for one half hour of your favorite tunes. You name them, We'll play them.

* * * * * * * * * * * * * * * * *

SERIOUS SIDE (cont from pg 1)

whether we live in the North or the South; whether we are Jew, Christian, or Atheist we must respect the rights and opinions of our fellow men, our fellow Americans. This is tolerance. If we have learned tolerance and practice it, life will be easier for us and those around us. If we have achieved this, then we can say with confidence that during our time in the service of the United States, we have become better and wiser.

* * * * * * * * * * * * * * * * *

LADY LUCKS SCUTTLEBUTT NEWS

Published with the cooperation of the men of the USS LST 864.
Editor: Bob Bell Y2c
Co Editor: Jule Swope GM2c
Cartoonist: Frank Bunker SC2c
Sports: Pat O'Brien GM2c
The Editors wish to express their appreciation to the men who have made this edition possible.

Scuttlebutt of October 5, 1945, page 4

```
                        ADDRESSES
                          OF THE
                          CREW
```

The men in the crew have been asking for the addresses of their shipmates for the last two months. Below are the names, addresses and home states compiled on 28 September 1945:

```
R. B. Wathen;       260 Cherokee Road;    Charlotte, North Carolina.
F. L. Haines;       315 E. Center;  Blanchester, Ohio.
W. R. Hanley;       3986 Murdock Ave;  New York City, New York.
E. P. Hanley;       3986 Murdock Ave;  New York City, New York.
L. P. Holmes Jr.;   P.O. Box 35;   Napa, California.
P. N. Wood;    35 Bowden Street;    Douglasville, Georgia
B. W. Gibson;   Box 8;    Seminary, Mississippi.
R. D. Peter Jr.;    R. D. #1;  Norristown, Penna.
W. R. Provins;    DeKalb, Texas.
L. N. Pitts Jr.;    Florence, Alabama.
C. O. Adams;    721 E. Chestnut,;   Louisville, 2, Ky.
E. E. Stotts;    Red Eagle Route;   Pawhask, Okla.
R. C. Regel;    114-18 107th Ave. Richmond Hill, Long Island, N.Y.
L. P. Wooster;    51 Park Blvd,;   Clementon, N. J.
R. L. Bell;   8 State Street;   Ossining, New York
M. A. Kaehler;   8917 Lamon Ave.;   Skokie, Ill.
J. W. Denton;   Coweta Box 121;   Coweta, Okla.
F. Bunker;   Terrace Ave.;   Pine Hill, New Jersey.
H. E. Bullington;   R.F.D. 2;   Atwood Tenn.
S.E. Carlton;    1310 Hampton Ave.;   Greensville, S. C.
J. W. Timpany;   Pride Road;   Auburn, Maine.
W.J. Mueller;    5032 Alaska Ave;   St. Louis, Mo.
J.P. Gainor;    409 Chestnut St.;   Coatsville, Pa.
R. Mitchell;    412-3rd Ave;   Columbus, Ga.
H. Bailey;    219 Grosscup Ave.;   Dunbor, West Va.
A. Plonka;    3323 W. 37th Place;   Chicago, Ill.
J. G. Dobesh;    Rt. 1 Box 33;   Willow River, Minn.
J. H. Womack;   Box 37;   Hahira, Ga.
H. G. Bittiker;    204 N. Jefferson;   Carrollton, Mo.
F. Dobes;   56129 So. Morgan St.;   Chicago, Ill.
J. R. Buckingham;   Edgerton Rd;   Brecksville, Ohio
R.W. Parker;   Town Line Road;   Mineral Ridge, Ohio.
N. McCloud;    250 W. 128th St.;   New York City, New York.
E. Crowell;    179 West River St.;   Providence, R. I.
D. F. Bartlett;    Slash Rd.;   Wilson, New York.
R. C. Ross;    912 Warrin Ave.;   Niles, Ohio
G. M. Jacobson;   Box 208;   Densmore, Kansas
J. H. Swope;   136 Carlisle;   Gettisberg, Penna.
L.C. Horner;   PO Box 222 Grabur Heights;   Graham, N. C.
E. W. Abderhalden;   9556 S. Albany;   Chicago, 42 Ill.
L. J. Parrick;    1004 Maine St.;   Quincy, Ill.
W.E. Bertouille;    1316 Ridge Ave.;   Steubenville; Ohio
R. G. Adair;   R. R. #1;   Danville, Ill.
J. H. Evans;    1401 Forrest Ave.;   Dallas, Tex.
J. V. Lipinski;   Monongah, W. Va.
D. Gay;   Doorway;   Kentucky.
R.L.Gregg;   179 Bartlett St.;   Asheville, N.C.
S.D. Flatt;   Palma Sola;   Flordia.
C.A. Utberg Jr.;   220 Center Ave;   Emsworth, Pgh (2) Pa.
H. Szerzinski;    2236 Dadier St.;   St. Louis, Mo.
J. Neal;    341 West Delaware;   Toledo Ohio.
L. Wick;   Kiel Route 1;   Schoolhill, Wisc.
D. W. Campbell;    R.R. 1;   West Parker Rd;   Greenville, S. C.
A. DiPalma;    205 South 3rd St.;   Steubenville, Ohio
```

                              PAGE FIVE

Scuttlebutt of October 5, 1945, page 5

ADDRESSES (continued)

D. Emmel; 371 Morado Dwellings; Beaver Falls Pa.
G.H. Leverett; 224 5th St.; Oakland, Calif.
J. W. Walling; Hamilton Missouri.
Pelkey; M. L.; 193rd & 55 N.E. Rt 6; Seattle, 55, Washington.
J. Hammond; 2145 Adelaide Ave; St. Louis, Mo.
S.M. Nagel; 202 Henry St.; New York, 2, New York.
N.C. May; 207 Ford St.; Fredericksburg, Va.
L. R. Murray; 18 Kendall St. Clifton Springs, N.Y.
J. H. Hugunin; RR 1; Linton, Indiana.
J. R. Holmes; 920-7th St. SW; B'ham, Ala.
H. L. Bausman; 40 So. Alder St.; Dayton, Ohio
L. S. Satterly; 315 Court St.; Laurenceburg, Ky.
W. O. Rushing; Big Sandy, Tenn.
J. H. Mullen; 22 Clare St.; Lowell Mass.
M. J. Lapham; 3034 So Annabelle; Detroit 25 Mich.
J. D. Crutchfield; Star Route; Kernersville, N. C.
J. J. Paulik; 631-14th St.; Oshkosh, Wisc.
J. N. Maher; Morristown; South Dak.
R. A. Berzinski; Galesville, Wisc.
L. W. Swazey; Brownville Junction, Maine.
W. E. Thomas; 101 E Bertsch St.; Lansford, Penna.
G. O. Rose; Box 205; Stone, Ky.
D. N. Ellis; 146 W. 5th St. Hartford, Ill.
D. L. Wever; Diranton, Iowa.
F.J. Burns; 131 W. Airy St. Norristown, Penna.
P. Loar; 23 N. Hazelwood Ave,; Newark, Pa.
T. Cox; RCD Box 132; Wichita Falls, Texas
J. M. Dunman Jr.; Box 142; Monroe City; Tex.
R. B. Miller; 905 So. College Ave.; Aledo, Ill.
C. Winters; 8125 Homer; Detroit, Mich.
V.R. Truesdale Jr.; PO Box 143, ; Cayce, S.C.
J.F. Zorich; 1130 Shotwell St.; San Francisco, Calif.
C. Storgaard; Irene, South Dak.
M. Dreese; Halstead Kansas.
A. Knutson, Bricelyn, Minn.
Prokop, A.; Box 774; Russellton, Pa.
H. O. Tinlin; RD 2; Carrollton, Ohio
P. Hogle; RD 2; Conneaut, Ohio
G.L. Lanchett; 35014 Ash St. Wayne, Mich.
E. Chambless; Star Pt. Box 138; Atmore Ala.
R.A. Knapp; 805 Van Brout; Kansas City, Mo.
W. Barrow; 277 East Harding Blvd, San Antonio Texas.
D. White; Box 7013; Asheville, N.C.
J. M. Shelton; Garrisonville, Va.
T.N. Thompson; Jamestown, N. C.
B. F. O'Brien; 41 Squire St.; Hartford, Conn.
W. K. Reeble; 101 Merchant; Emporia, Kans.
W. H. Robins; 6113 Clover Lane; Richmond Va.
H.P. Dever; 501 W 32nd St.; Chicago, Ill.
J.A. Terry; R 2 Box 602; Pine Bluff, Ark.

PAGE SIX

Scuttlebutt of October 5, 1945, page 6

THE STRANGE LADY

She had a certain warmth about her. Perhaps I'm just prejudice, but when I saw her standing there on the beach, her glistening body vibrant with life, and the waves splashing against her back, falling the length of her firm bottom - well, I knew that I'd never be satisfied with another. Those were busy times; Japan was felling for peace, & I had been so busy that I hadn't thought of her 'till Tuesday, my day off. Afternoons off were hard to get. Something drew me to the beach that afternoon, but the feeling was new and strange - left me vacant. When I saw her I knew she wasn't mine. She wasnt married; I knew this, but she was loaded.

It didn't exactly take away from the beauty of her shape. She protruded a little on top, but her carriage was splendid, & the smoothness of her back blended with the firmness of her bottom. Yet within her I knew that she carried a strange lifeless thing that was bound for life in a new & foreign land. I tried to talk to her, let my hand fall along the length of her side, to come to rest on her bottom. When she moves she quivered with every touch; as she lay in the water, she seemed a part of the sea itself. As I lay on her, I let my hand run the length of her suit. Then it seemed as though I could see through her; her with her well rounded body. She looked just a little haggard, and her paint was coming off. It was then that she told me she was going to Japan to get rid of her load. When she told me how many men were going to ride her on the trip there, how many men were keeping her, I felt as though the universal happiness being delt out as a fift of world peace would surely never reach my heart. Yet I knew that she satisfied my every physical desire; I had to live with her sleep with her, feel her quiver underneath. On Thursday, 23rd August we left Pearl Harbor for Japan. I knew that within a few months she would give birth to this lifeless creature she carried. Then with a new paint job, she would be more beautiful than ever. Hers is the beauty of the sea, a restless, lively beauty seen only by men who go down to the sea in ships. She has no name, no home; but she's a lady to her very bottom, "Lady Luck"..

* * * * * * * * * * * * *

HERE-AFTER

A young girl wanted her boy friend to talk about the here-after. He said, "if you are not here-after what I'm here-after you'll be here-after I'm gone".

INSTRUCTIONS FOR THE USE OF THE NEW DIAL TELEPHONE SYSTEM

The letters on the dial are sometimes confusing to the average layman. The letter S on the dial is for South; the letter P is the Parkdale; the letter O is for Operator. Now if you want South Parkdale; you put your finger in the S hole, then you put your finger in the P hole.

If you don't get your party, put your finger in the Operator's hole and move finger back and forth gently until the Operator comes; then you will be able to make connections, providing you don't go off until the Operator comes.

* * * * * * * * * * * * *

HOW TO WORK A MOTOR HIGH-SPEED

Husband (at telephone) - Hello, give me 133 please. Is that Dr. Smith?

Dr. Smith - Yes, Sir.

Husband - Say, doctor, my wife is very ill, seems all run down. What do you advise me to do to her. (At that time the telephone clerk cut the husband off from the doctor and connected him with a salesman who was telling a customer how to make a motor washer go better).

Salesman to husband - Draw her water off, give her time to cool, take her jacket off and feel her bottom, then blow her flue out, get hot again, then try her backwards, and if she is no better, let some other man have a go at her. - Ring off please!

* * * * * * * * * * * * *

WATCH YOUR KNEE

It seems that a lady went to the doctors & asked him the best way to comit suicide. The doctor told her that she was very upset and to forget the idea. The lady said that if he didn't tell her a good way, she would jump off a 60 story building. Finally the doctor gave in and told her to go home, undress, go to bed and shoot herself below the right breast. She went home, undressed, went to bed and blew off her right kneecap.

* * * * * * * * * *

Scott's tissue (It's Soft).

Used by Admirals and seaman alike. Try the large econimical size or the handy dandy junior size. If you are traveling, take with you the postage stamp size for convenience sake. But, use rubber g[loves]

Scuttlebutt of October 5, 1945, page 7

LADY LUCK'S SCUTTLEBUTT

We print only the news that's fit to print

WEATHER: Rough Seas, calming down sometime in the future.

Published November 26th, 1945 at sea by and for the men of the USS LST 864. Vol. I No. 4

"LADY" HOMEWARD BOUND!

"MINE SUNK, SCRATCH ONE"...

While underway from Sasebo, Japan to Pearl Harbor on the morning of November 20th, on or about 1000, the lookout sighted a mine. All Gunner's Mates were immediately called to the bow with their 30 cal. rifles and ammunition. The ship maneuvered into position for firing. Wondering why all the gunner's mates were called to the bow most of the crew came topside. The ship was maneuvered within 200 yards of the mine and the order to commence firing was given.

Approximately 35 to 40 rounds were fired when there came a terrific explosion, and all hands hit the deck and dove for cover when shrapnel and water started to fall. When the effects of the concussion had disappeared and dead fish began to appear on the surface of the angry waters (there were swells ranging from 15 to 30 feet high), we backed away from the scene and resumed our base course for Pearl. The radioman on watch then related over the SCR to the OTC, "sighted mine, sank same".

* * * * * * * * * * * * * * * *

RELIEVING OF COMMAND

On October 27th, 1945, Lieutenant Richard B. Nathan was relieved of his command of the USS LST 864 and Ensign Frank L. Haines, assumed full command. Lt(jg) R. O. Peter Jr. assumed the position as Executive Officer, Ensign J. W. Roll and assumed the position as Engineering Officer. All other officers assumed their regular duties.

Underway from Sasebo, Kyushu, Japan for Pearl Harbor T. H., LLSBN: 1000:

Need we say more! Our dreams and prayers have been answered after long last, and we are now leaving our sullen faced Japanese people, brown skinned natives, grass huts, palm trees, sandy beaches, and what have you behind us as we tread our way from Sasebo Japan to Pearl Harbor, T. H. for further routing to the good old Uncle Sugar.

Upon leaving Leyte Gulf, in the Philippines, we were ordered to Subic Bay, Luzon to pick up troops for further routing. Our hope of the States vanished; we settled down to what we thought would be another 8 to 10 months of this beautiful vast blue Pacific. We were carrying aboard as passengers, 35 Philippine Guerrillas, most of whom were in the famous "death march" on Bataan. Upon arriving at Subic Bay, a Sub Chaser pulled up alongside and the passengers disembarked. We were then ordered to proceed to Lingayen Gulf, Luzon for further orders. Ahh, Lingayen Gulf; with it's quaint straw and swaying palm trees, its never ending rice patties and speaking of rice patties........We'll talk about same other time. We loaded our tank deck and main deck with supplies and equipment and men of the Army Quartermaster Unit, on the shore of Agno Beach below the city of Baggiyo, the city in the clouds. After completing our loading operations, we were ordered to report to Sasebo Naval Base on Kyushu, Japan. The 8 day trip from Luzon was pretty rough, running into the tail-end of a small typhoon and strong winds. We made Sasebo Bay 25 October and unloaded the Army Quartermasters on a Jap Seaplane ramp. There was a large number of Jap Seaplanes and Zero's piled up on the beach and a few nights later, flame throwers set them off. It made a beautiful sight to see the once proud Jap airforce paying part of it's debt for December 7th. Our stay in Sasebo was long and drawn out and most of the crew getting restless, but on the 13th of October, around 1100, the word was passed over the P.A. for all hand to lay up to the main deck for quarters for muster. Men tripped down ladders forming divisions and after a few short moments, our division officers told us that "We have received orders to report to Pearl Harbor for onward routing." At 0800 the following morning, we weighed anchor for Pearl Harbor, without sparing the horses. This is it!!!

Scuttlebutt of November 26, 1945, page 1

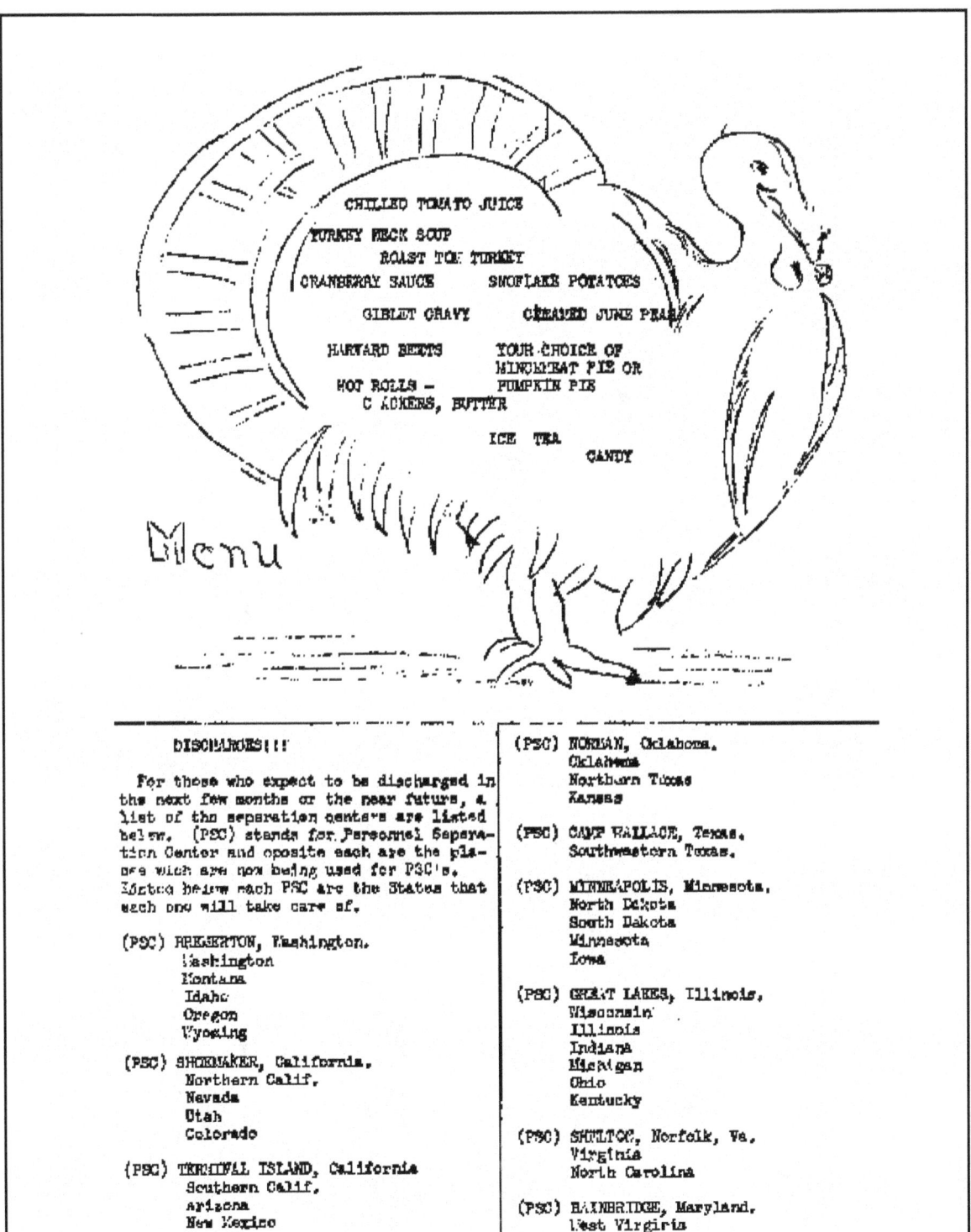

Menu

CHILLED TOMATO JUICE
TURKEY NECK SOUP
ROAST TOM TURKEY
CRANBERRY SAUCE   SNOFLAKE POTATOES
GIBLET GRAVY   CREAMED JUNE PEAS
HARVARD BEETS   YOUR CHOICE OF
               MINCEMEAT PIE OR
HOT ROLLS —   PUMPKIN PIE
CRACKERS, BUTTER
ICE TEA
CANDY

DISCHARGES!!!

For those who expect to be discharged in the next few months or the near future, a list of the separation centers are listed below. (PSC) stands for Personnel Separation Center and oposite each are the places which are now being used for PSC's. Listed below each PSC are the States that each one will take care of.

(PSC) BREMERTON, Washington.
    Washington
    Montana
    Idaho
    Oregon
    Wyoming

(PSC) SHOEMAKER, California.
    Northern Calif.
    Nevada
    Utah
    Colorado

(PSC) TERMINAL ISLAND, California
    Southern Calif.
    Arizona
    New Mexico
    West Texas

(cont. in next column)

PAGE TWO

(PSC) NORMAN, Oklahoma.
    Oklahoma
    Northern Texas
    Kansas

(PSC) CAMP WALLACE, Texas.
    Southwestern Texas.

(PSC) MINNEAPOLIS, Minnesota.
    North Dakota
    South Dakota
    Minnesota
    Iowa

(PSC) GREAT LAKES, Illinois.
    Wisconsin
    Illinois
    Indiana
    Michigan
    Ohio
    Kentucky

(PSC) SHELTON, Norfolk, Va.
    Virginia
    North Carolina

(PSC) BAINBRIDGE, Maryland.
    West Virginia
    Maryland
    Eastern Penn.
    Delaware

Cont. on page THREE

Scuttlebutt of November 26, 1945, page 2

BOOK OF THE MONTH
"THE DARK STRANGER"
by
Constance W. Dodge

There is a magnificient sweep to the action of this novel. It begins in the bloody days of 1745, in Scotland when the blindly loyal clansman followed Prince Charles, rebel heir to the throne, to destruction. It carries through days of struggle and bloodshed in the American Colonies, to the final destiny of the dark stranger.

The dark stranger is Dugald McLean, who was a child during the Scottish rebellion, and with his father and brother, fled to Carahna. Always a stranger, his restless feet carried him from a secure plantation, through Indian wars and eventually to sea under John Paul Jones. Always in search of something vital to his way of life which he himself could not clearly grasp.

The climax is reached when he finds that missing link to his every way of life. Something we have every day, but never realize, nor do we appreciate how important it is. If you like Historical novels blended into a fictional tale, by all means read "The Dark Stranger".

* * * * * * * * * * * * * * * * * * * *

DISCHARGES (Cont. from page TWO)

(PSC) SAMPSON, New York.
Northwestern New York
Western Penn.

(PSC) LIDO BEACH, Long Island.
New Jersey
Connecticut
Eastern New York.

(PSC) BOSTON, Mass.
Rhode Island.
Massachussetts.
Vermont
New Hampshire
Maine.

(PSC) TOLEDO, Ohio.
Northern Ohio.

(PSC) ST. LOUIS, Mo.
Nebraska
Missouri

(PSC) MEMPHIS, Tennessee.
Arkansas
Northern Mississippi
Northern Alabama
Tennessee

(PSC) NEW ORLEANS, La.
Northwestern Florida
Southern Mississippi
Southern Alabama
Louisiana

(PSC) JACKSONVILLE, Florida.
All but Northwestern Florida
Georgia

(PSC) CHARLESTON, S. C.
South Carolina.

* * * * * * * * * * * * * * * * * *

"28 SHOPPING DAYS LEFT TILL CHRISTMAS"

Don't delay another day, make your shopping lists early this year. Our ship's Service has a variety of toys for the kiddies; men's apparel and a assorted selection of shaving creams, candy bars (now 3 for 10¢) and double edge blades for the women. Open evenings anywhere from 1600 to 1630.

Scuttlebutt of November 26, 1945, page 3

LADY LUCK'S TRAVELOGUE

October 7th, 1944	Crew was formed for 4 weeks of training at the Amphibious Training Base, Camp Bradford, NorVa.
October 21, 1944	Two weeks training cruise on the Chesapeak Bay on the LST 683.
November 15, 1944	Left Camp Bradford for Chicago, Ill. Upon arrival at Navy Pier Chicago, a nucleus crew was formed to proceed to Jeffersonville Indiana for pre-commissioning and the remainder of the crew was to proceed to Great Lakes, Ill. for gunnery training.
December 7, 1944	Total crew aboard the 864 for sailing down the Mississippi River to New Orleans La. for commissioning ceremonies.
December 13, 1944	Commissioned at New Orleans (Algiers) La.
December 20, 1944	Underway from New Orleans (Algiers) La. to Panama City, St. Andrews Bay Florida for shakedown exercises, in the Gulf of Mexico
December 22, 1944	Dropped anchor in St. Andrews Bay Fla. Shakedown period began.
January 4, 1945	Underway from St. Andrew Bay Fla. to New Orleans La.
January 5, 1945	Moored at Ship Yards in New Orleans La. Took aboard Army Passengers and also LCT 1428 was hoisted aboard the main deck.
January 16, 1945	Underway from New Orleans (Algiers) La. to the Panama Canal Zone via the Carribbean Sea.
January 22, 1945	Arrived at Coco Solo Panama, disembarked army personnel and continued through the Canal Locks.
January 23, 1945	Moored at Balboa, Canal Zone.
January 26, 1945	Underway from Panama Canal Zone to San Diego, Calif.
February 7, 1945	Moored at Naval Repair Base, San Diego, Calif.
February 12, 1945	Underway from San Diego, Calif. to Port Hueneme, Calif. for pontoons.
February 13, 1945	Underway from Port Hueneme, Calif. to Seattle Washington.
February 19, 1945	Moored at Seattle Washington preparing to take aboard Army personnel.
February 26, 1945	Underway from Seattle Washington to Pearl Harbor, T. H.
March 9, 1945	Arrived Pearl Harbor, T. H.
March 13, 1945	Underway from Pearl Harbor, T. H. to Eniwetok, Marshall Islands
March 24, 1945	Anchored at Eniwetok, Marshall Islands.
March 25, 1945	Underway from Eniwetok, Marshalls to Guam, Marianas Islands.
March 29, 1945	Anchored at Guam, Marianas Islands.
March 30, 1945	Underway from Guam, Marianas to Ulithi, Caroline Islands.
April 1, 1945	Anchored off Mog Mog Island, Ulithi, Caroline Islands.
April 12, 1945	Underway from Ulithi, Carolines to Okinawa Jima, Ryukyus Islan
April 18, 1945	Arrived in Nago Wan Harbor, Okinawa Jima.
April 22, 1945	Beached on IE Shima, Okinawa Gunto, Ryukyus Islands. Unloaded Army personnel.
April 26, 1945	Launched Pontoons and LCT 1428 in Hagushi Bay.
April 29, 1945	Underway from Naha, Okinawa Jima to Ulithi, Caroline Islands.
May 5, 1945	Arrived Ulithi Harbor, Carolines.
May 18, 1945	Underway from Ulithi, Carolines to Leyte, Philippines.
May 20, 1945	Arrived San Pedro Bay, Leyte, Philippine Islands. Received aboard Army personnel.
June 7, 1945	Underway from Leyte, Philippine Islands to Kerama Retto, Ryuky
June 12, 1945	Anchored in Kerama Retto, Ryukyus Islands.
June 12, 1945	Underway from Kerama Retto to Okinawa Jima.
June 13, 1945	Anchored in Hagushi Bay, Okinawa Jima, Ryukyus. Unloaded Army personnel and equipment.
June 18, 1945	Underway from Okinawa Jima to Saipan, Marianas Islands.
June 24, 1945	Anchored in Saipan Harbor, Saipan, Marianas Islands.
July 21, 1945	Underway from Saipan to Pearl Harbor, T. H.
August 5, 1945	Arrived Pearl Harbor, T.H. Received pontoons and Navy personnel
August 24, 1945	Departed Pearl Harbor, T.H. enroute Eniwetok, Marshall Islands.
August 25, 1945	Changed orders and proceeded to Midway Island, T. H.
August 30, 1945	Arrived Midway Island, T. H.
August 30, 1945	Underway from Midway to Yokosuka Naval Base, Japan.
September 10, 1945	Arrived Yokosuka Japan and unloaded Navy occupational troops.
September 27, 1945	Underway from Yokosuka, Japan to Leyte, Philippines.
October 5, 1945	Arrived Leyte Gulf, Philippine Islands. Received aboard 35 Philippine passengers.

Scuttlebutt of November 26, 1945, page 4

LADY LUCK'S TRAVELOGUE - Continued -

October 12, 1945........Underway for Subic Bay, Luzon, Philippines. Upon arrival at Subic Bay, we disembarked the 35 Philippine passengers and our orders were changed to proceed to San Fernando, Lingayen Gulf, Luzon.

October 16, 1945........Arrived San Fernando, Luzon.

October 18, 1945........Received aboard Army personnel and equipment for passage from Lingayen Gulf, Luzon to Sasebo Naval Base, Sasebo Japan.

October 25, 1945........Arrived Sasebo Japan.

November 14, 1945......Departed Sasebo Ko, Kyushu, Japan enroute to Pearl Harbor for further routing to the Uncle Sugar.

A SAILOR'S DREAM
by T.N. Thompson

I gazed at the beach ahead -
T'was a beautiful place we were headed for -
I couldn't enjoy the scenery,
Because I knew just what was in store.

G.Q. soon was sounded -
We manned every one of our guns -
Some said it was tragic,
And a few - said it was great fun.

Bursting shells filled the air -
They kept us awake all night
Wishing, hoping and praying,
That this would end up the fight.

Perhaps we are a bunch of kids -
But brother, we know the score -
We worship and love our four freedoms
And that's what were fighting for.

Slowly we fought on -
Making one beach-head after another -
Hoping each would be the last,
And we could go home to Mother.

Now, the war is won -
My dream has almost come true -
Don't worry, dear Mother,
I'll soon be home with you.

LADY LUCKS SCUTTLEBUTT NEWS

Published with the cooperation of the men of the USS LST 864.
Editor: Bob Bell Y2c
Co Editor: Jule Swope QM2c
Cartoonist: Frank Bunker SC2c
Sports: Doug Campbell S1c
The Editors wish to express their appreciation to the men who have this editorial possible.

SPORT HI-LITES
(Basketball)

After a tough three week schedule at Sasebo, Japan, the ship's team has taken time out for a few weeks of rest. While they averaged two to three games a day, & were only defeated once by the LST 130, which they later defeated twice by a large margin. Now their win and lost column stands; 57 wins and 2 losses. "Big Irish Lipinski" and Captain "El Tiger" Haines are still playing great offensive as well as defensive. As usual, Ensign "Perry" Holmes is still racking up points with that ever faithful right hand shot of his. With the return of Ensign Jack Holland the team has been greatly strenghtened. Little Jack Horner is still playing that standing guard, as no one else can play it, and is always giving the opponents a headache.

A second team which was organized while at Sasebo, had a very victorious stay at Japan. They played 15 games and only suffered one loss. The "Wash-woman", Bittiker and his famous snowbird shot upheld the majority of the points. The Third-Birds, Bailey, as well as the rest of the team, played splendid ball.

In the intermural league, the Third-Birds still held first place with 11 wins and 1 loss, the loss being handed to them by the Officers in a very close game. Third-Birds suffered a great loss when Shelton, QM2c, recently left the ship. Irish Lipinski is still playing his swell brand of ball and is at the top of the Third-Birds scoring list.

Wash-woman Bittiker better known in the basketball world as "Greasy-black-Ace is the leading league scorer. With an average of 12½ points per game.

(Football)

During the recreation parties spent on the shores of Sasebo, Japan football and baseball games were enjoyed by most of the crew. Due to returns not being turned in, we have no account of the scores made at the games.

Scuttlebutt of November 26, 1945, page 5

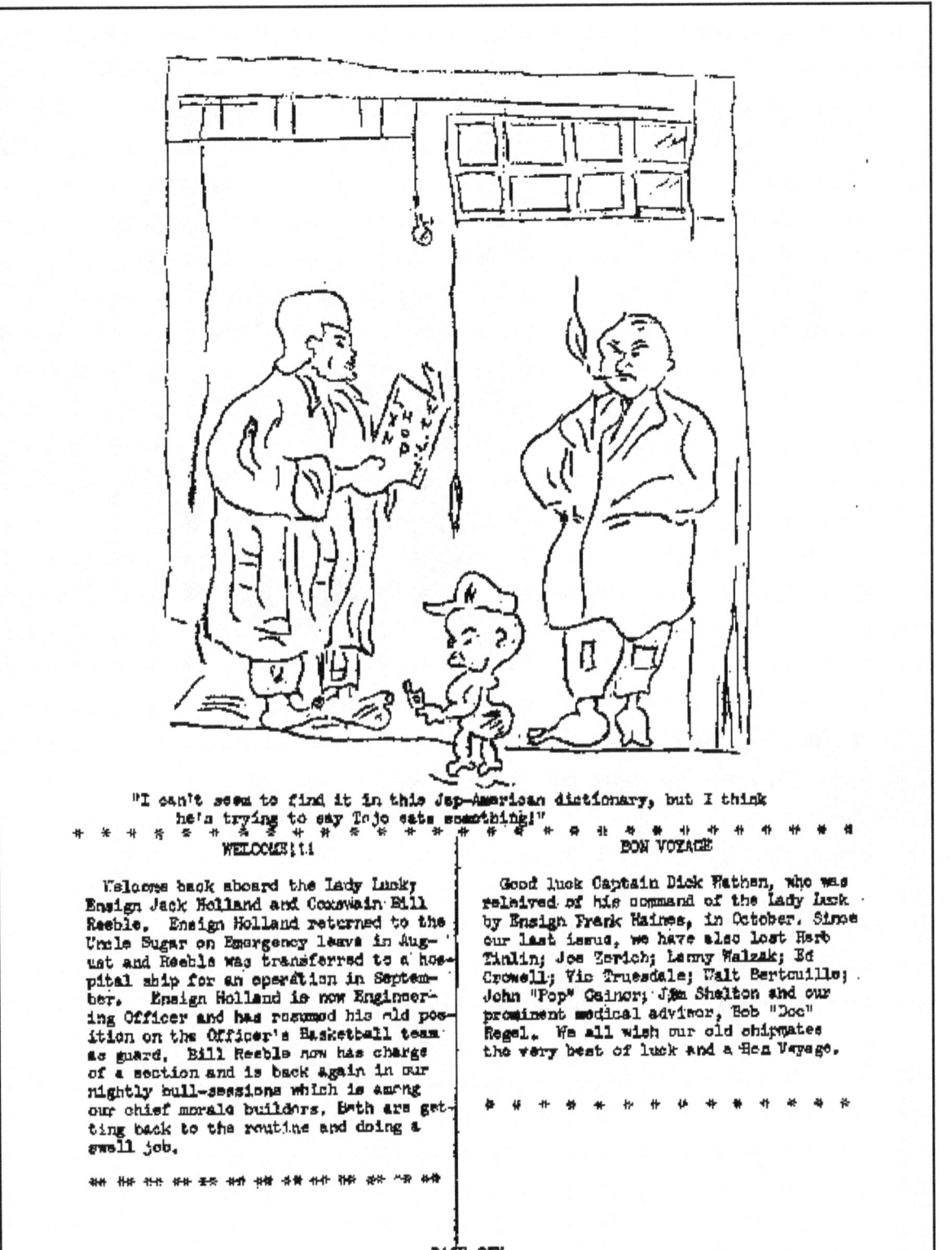

"I can't seem to find it in this Jap-American dictionary, but I think he's trying to say Tojo eats something!"

* *

WELCOME!!!

Welcome back aboard the Lady Lucky Ensign Jack Holland and Coxswain Bill Reeble. Ensign Holland returned to the Uncle Sugar on Emergency leave in August and Reeble was transferred to a hospital ship for an operation in September. Ensign Holland is now Engineering Officer and has resumed his old position on the Officer's Basketball team as guard. Bill Reeble now has charge of a section and is back again in our nightly bull-sessions which is among our chief morale builders. Both are getting back to the routine and doing a swell job.

BON VOYAGE

Good luck Captain Dick Wathen, who was relieved of his command of the Lady Luck by Ensign Frank Haines, in October. Since our last issue, we have also lost Herb Tinlin; Joe Zerich; Lenny Walzak; Ed Crowell; Vic Truesdale; Walt Bertouille; John "Pop" Gainor; Jim Shelton and our prominent medical adviser, Bob "Doc" Regel. We all wish our old shipmates the very best of luck and a Bon Voyage.

PAGE SIX

Scuttlebutt of November 26, 1945, page 6

Carlo Martin Jacobson (left), Glen Oval "Rosie" Rose, and Unknown

H. E. Bullington (left) and an unnamed buddy

CHAPTER 5

WAR DIARY OF LST GROUP NINETY-ONE

The declassified confidential records shown on the following pages make it clear that the men who served on the LST-864 were regularly in harm's way during the war in the Pacific. LSTs, routinely referred to as *Large Slow Targets*, would have been a prized kill for Japanese aircraft or warships or submarines, since they were often heavily laden with men, munitions, and various kinds of vehicles and equipment. For this reason, they normally traveled in convoy and were heavily protected by escorts.

The men were also in constant danger of accidents aboard these crowded, cargo-laden ships. LSTs were notoriously unstable and rough-riding vessels in bad weather, enough so that on repeated occasions the men were scared half to death that equipment might break loose or that they might sink in the middle of a severe storm. Some of the crewmen, in fact, were more scared more by one particular typhoon than they ever were by the Japanese. An account of the damage done by this typhoon is included, just for the sake of illustrating how harmful and dangerous these storms could be.

~~SECRET~~ DECLASSIFIED

WAR DIARY
LST GROUP NINETY-ONE

JANUARY 16-31	1945	- 104807
FEBRUARY 1-28	1945	- 110702
MARCH 1-31	1945	- 114315
APRIL 1-30	1945	- 120067
MAY 1-31	1945	- 124402
JUNE 1-30	1945	- 131421
JULY 1-31	1945	- 136024
AUGUST 1-31	1945	- 144827
SEPTEMBER 1-30	1945	- 151437
OCTOBER 1-31	1945	- 151438
NOVEMBER 1-30	1945	- 154601
(Missing)		
FEBRUARY 1-28	1945	- 121826
MARCH 1-31	1945	- 121826
APRIL 1-30	1945	- 121826
MAY 1-31	1945	- 124304
JUNE 1-30	1945	- 128594
JULY 1-31	1945	- 155535
AUGUST 1-31	1945	- 140345
SEPTEMBER 1-30	1945	- 146430
OCTOBER 1-31	1945	- 152581
NOVEMBER 1-30	1945	- 152581

San Francisco, Calif.

LST 864/A12-1
Serial: 02

1 February 1945

CONFIDENTIAL

From: Commanding Officer.
To: Commander in Chief United States Fleet.

Subject: War Diary, Month of 1 February 1945.

1 February to 6 February.

Steaming enroute to San Diego, Calif. from Balboa, Canal Zone. We are steaming independantly, carrying one third cargo of radio supplies. Our orders go as far as San Diego only. We are carrying LCT 1428 placed on the main deck at New Orleans, La.

7 February to 11 February.

We are moored in San Diego Harbor discharging cargo and taking on supplies.

12 February.

Underway enroute for Port Hueneme, Calif. from San Diego, Calif. to take on pontoons.

13 February to 18 February.

Underway enroute from Port Hueneme, Calif. to Seattle Washington,

19 February to 25 February.

Anchored in Seattle Harbor. We joined up with LST Group 91 under command of Commander J. H. Motes, aboard LST 854. We took combat Engineers of the 1903rd Division aboard with equipment. We fueled, watered, and provisioned as ordered.

26 February to 28 February.

Underway enroute to Pearl Harbor from Seattle, Washington steaming in single two column formation.

cc: Cincpac
ComLSTGr69

R. B. Wathen, Lieut, USNR
Commanding.

```
                              San Francisco, Calif.
LST 864/A12-1                                    1 March 1945
Serial: 03

CONFIDENTIAL

From:      Commanding Officer.
To:        Commander in Chief United States Fleet.

Subject:   War Diary, Month of March 1945.
```

1 March to 8 March.

    Steaming enroute from Seattle Washington to Pearl Harbor in company with LST Group 91 under Command of Commander J. H. Motes, USN aboard LST 854. Zone description plus 7.5 in use. The Group is carrying combat Engineers of 1903rd division, with equipment, to foward area for assignment to duty. No orders have been issued as regards combat mission.

9 March to 12 March.

    Moored in Berth Tare 11, Pearl Harbor.

13 March to 23 March.

    Steaming enroute to Eniwetok, Marshall Islands, from Pearl Harbor; no escort vessels present.

24 March.

    Anchored at Eniwetok, Marshall Islands.

25 March to 28 March.

    Steaming enroute from Eniwetok, Marshall Islands to Guam, Marianas Islands; no escort vessels present.

29 March.

    Anchored in Apra Harbor, Guam, Marianas Islands.

30 March to 31 March.

    Steaming enroute from Guam, Marianas Islands to Ulithi, Caroline Islands; no escort vessels present.

121826

                                               R. B. Wathen, Lieut, USNR
                                               Commanding.

cc: Cincpac
     ComLSTGr69

WAR DIARY OF LST GROUP NINETY-ONE

S-E-C-R-E-T

LST GROUP 91, FLOTILLA 31
C/O FLEET POST OFFICE
SAN FRANCISCO, CALIFORNIA

1 April 1945

L.S.T. GROUP NINETY-ONE
Aboard U.S.S. LST 854

Steaming as before. 0500 sighted Ulithi Atoll, Western Carolines. 0900 formed single column before starting in channel. 1030 first ship of T.U. 13.11.7 anchored. 1130 all ships completed anchoring in Northern anchorages, Ulithi Atoll. Reported to ComPhibsPac for duty by dispatch Serial No. 011312 of April.

2 April 1945 - 9 April 1945.

Anchored as before in Northern Anchorage, Ulithi Atoll, Western Carolines in berths 2, 26, and 101 awaiting further orders from ComPhibsPac.

10-11 April 1945.

Anchored as before.

12 April 1945.

Anchored as before. At 1500 all ships this Task Unit, 94.18.13, including LSTs 854(Flagship), 874, 825, 840, 863, 960, 957, 864, 837, 841, 836; 822, 843, 821, LSM 90, USS AZIMECH, AK 124, USS ARMADILLO IX111, USS ARISTAEUS, ARB 1, USS MAHOGANY AN23, SS CAPE SAN MARTIN, and SS CAPE ISABEL, with 5 escorts consisting of USS STERN DE 187, (Screen Commander), USS CROSBY APD 17, USS RATHBURNE, APD 25, USS O'NEILL DE 188, and USS PAUL G BAKER DE 642, under command of Commander J. H. MOTES, U.S. Navy. Underway from Ulithi Harbor, Western Carolines, to join up in convoy in obedience to sailing orders from Port Director, Ulithi, dated 12 April 1945, enroute Okinawa, Ryukyus. At 1800 all ships completed forming up and taking proper stations, and course set for destination.

Positions

	2000
Lat.	10°-19'N
Long.	139°-45'E

13 April 1945

Steaming as before.

positions

	0800	1200	2000
Lat.	11°-58'N	12°-11'N	13°-13'N
Long.	138°-59'E	138°-28'E	137°-39'E

5 978

Fleet Post Office
San Francisco, Calif.

LST 864/A12-1
Serial: 04

1 April 1945

CONFIDENTIAL

From: Commanding Officer.
To: Commander in Chief United States Fleet.

Subject: War Diary, Month of April 1945.

1 April to 11 April.

Anchored in Ulithi Anchorage, Carolines Islands in company with LST Group 91 under command of Commander J. H. Motes, USN aboard LST 854. Aboard LST's of this group are the combat Engineers of 1903rd Division; Group is awaiting the assignment of a combat mission. Zone description minus 10 is in use.

11 April to 17 April.

Steaming enroute from Ulithi, Caroline Islands to Okinawa Gunto with various fleet units comprising task unit 94.18.13 under command of Commander J. H. Motes, USN aboard LST 854, six escort vessels present. The task unit is in simple convoy formation; our ship is steaming in position 34.

18 April.

At 0800 we arrived off southern coast of Okinawa. The task unit separated and LST's of Group 91 proceeded up the west coast. At 1400, we anchored in Nago Wan. at 2030, we were ordered to make smoke. Although no enemy aircraft were sighted, heavy anti aircraft fire was visible off Hagushi.

19 April.

Anchored as before in Nago Wan.

20 April.

At 1330, we departed Nago Wan for IE Shima. Arriving at IE Shima at 1800 we stood off shore awaiting orders to beach and commence unloading cargo.

121826

-1-

LST 864/A12-1
CONFIDENTIAL Serial: 04   1 April 1945

Subject: War Diary, Month of April 1945.

21 April.

At 0130, we went to General Quarters with orders to fire on unidentified aircraft, none were seen. At 0145 we were ordered to make smoke. At 0200, we secured from General Quarters. No action occurred during the day. At 2000, we went to General Quarters; secured at 2130. No enemy planes were sighted.

22 April.

At 0100, ship went to General Quarters; we secured at 0130, no enemy planes seen. At 1430 we got underway for unloading operations on IE Shima. The entrance through coral reef to the beaching area was treacherous. The ship was beached at 1545, and unloading operations proceeded. Vehicles were rolled off first. At 2030, sniper shots were reported striking the pontoons.

23 April.

At 0200 we went to General Quarters, but sighted no enemy planes. Unloading completed, we retracted at 0700 and anchored off beach. At 1300, we steamed south to Hagushi, Okinawa, where we anchored at 1445 awaiting orders to launch LCT and pontoons.

24 April.

No Night action occurred. At 1400 we steamed north to IE Shima to pick up personnel to launch pontoons.

25 April.

No night action. At 0600, we steamed south to Nago Wan where we made preparations to launch our pontoons. Pontoons were launched at 1400.

26 April.

Anchored at Nago Wan, no night action. At 0630 we steamed south to Nagusni to launch LCT. At 1100 we launched LCT persuant to dispatch order number 250612 from CTG 51.21.

-2-

LST 864/A12-1
Serial: 04   CONFIDENTIAL   1 April 1945

Subject: War Diary, Month of April 1945.

27 April.

No night action from 0000 to sunrise. Our mission completed, we are awaiting orders to retire to rear area. At 2030 we went to General Quarters; sighted unidentified plane off stern at an estimated distance of 2800 yards, flying at about 500 feet elevation. Our #6 40MM fired four rounds at the target. The target disappeared; apparently no hits were obtained.

28 April.

At 0015, we went to General Quarters. At 0245 a Japanese "Betty" was sighted overhead. All guns commenced firing. The AA fire was heavy over the beach; all ships in the area were firing on the target. Those ships more than 500 yards from the beach were out of range, but continued firing. The "Betty" was out of range within 10 seconds. We expended 250 rounds of 20MM ammunition. There was no action during the day. At 2030 we again went to General Quarters. At 2200 a Japanese "Betty" made a bombing run over the beach, dropping three incendary bombs. We opened fire with our bow 40MM gun. The "Betty" got away. While all attention was attracted to this bombing run, another "Betty" came in low from seaward. She was immediately brought under fire by ships anchored about 8000 yards from the beach. The "Betty" was hit; she burst into flames and crashed into the water 2000 yards off our starboard beam. She did not release her bombs. We expended 55 rounds of 40MM ammunition.

29 April.

At 0200 we went to General Quarters. At 0230, a Japanese "Betty" made a bombing run on the beach, dropped two incendary bombs, and headed seaward. We brought the target under fire. The AA fire was so heavy that we were unable to tell if the plane was shot down; she quickly disappeared. We expended 150 rounds of 40MM ammunition, and 250 rounds of 20MM ammunition. There was no more action. At 0800 we steamed south to form up with task unit 51.29.25 under command of Commander J. H. Motes, USN, aboard LST 854. We departed Okinawa Gunto enroute to Ulithi, Carolines for repairs. We started steaming in simple convoy formation; our position was 54. There were three escort vessels.

30 April.

Steaming as before.

-3-

LST 864/A12-1
CONFIDENTIAL Serial: 04   1 April 1945.

Subject: War Diary, Month of April 1945.

Comment:

   During the Okinawa Gunto operations, the following points were noted by this command: During every air attack, all ships were ordered to make smoke; small boats circled around the bigger ships. This smoke reduced surface visibility so that an airplane was not visible at 1000 feet; yet the smoke was made so erradically that many ships were caught in open pockets of smoke, plainly visible from an airplane. The MK 14 sight was useless in the smoke. The percent of accuracy of AA fire was practically zero.

   It was also noted that most ships fired at the targets that were obviously out of range of all small auxiliaries having 20MM and 40MM only. Perhaps this was just the freshman desire of ships new to the combat area to fire on the enemy; they succeeded merely in increasing the volume of AA fire over our own ships, and everything that goes up must come down. Many of our personnel were injured by our own AA Shrapnel during the Okinawa operations.

   Smoke is and has been a great asset, but it's use is governed by the situation. Perhaps small auxiliaries would not waste so much ammunition in shooting at targets out of range would larger units transmit sufficient CIC information over a voice circuit guarded by smaller vessels.

cc: Cincpac
    ComLSTGr69

                                            R. B. Wathen, Lieut, USNR,
                                            Commanding.

APPROXIMATE MILAGE - Voyage of LST 864 from Seattle, Washington to Okinawa

Seattle to Hawaii - 2409 miles

Hawaii to Eniwetok - 2375 miles

Eniwetok to Guam - 1066 miles

Guam to Ulithi - 458 miles

Ulithi to Okinawa - 1260 miles

Barrage balloons above a convoy of LSTs. The ships were being loaded with troops and equipment for invasion. Barrage balloons provided protective covering against enemy aircraft and were often employed, although they were not used by LST-864.

Releasing weather balloons at sea

Photograph of LCT-831 being loaded on LST-864, a tricky maneuver. LCTs (Landing Craft, Tanks) were smaller than LSTs (Landing Ship, Tanks).

Lady Luck in a convoy of LSTs, heavily loaded with equipment and bound for the occupation of Japan after VJ Day. Note the movie screen in the foreground.

NATURAL DANGER AT SEA

One of the most memorable examples of the fury of Mother Nature to affect the USS LST-864 was the typhoon that hit the ship and many other navy ships (including those of the Japanese) on October 5 of 1945. As a means of stressing the fear that bad weather could inspire on hastily constructed and generally awkward to navigate ships such as the LSTs, a full account of the storm is presented in the pages that follow.

It was first spotted on October 4, 1945, developing in the Caroline Islands and tracked as it moved on a predictable course to the northwest. Although expected to pass into the East China Sea north of Formosa on 8 October, the storm unexpectedly veered north toward Okinawa. That evening the storm slowed down and, just as it approached Okinawa, began to greatly increase in intensity.

The sudden shift of the storm caught many ships and small craft in the constricted waters of Buckner Bay (Nakagusuku Wan) and they were unable to escape to sea. On October 9, when the storm passed over the island, winds of 80 knots (92 miles per hour) and 30 to 35-foot waves battered the ships and craft in the bay and tore into the quonset huts and buildings ashore. A total of 12 ships and craft were sunk, 222 grounded, and 32 severely damaged. Personnel casualties were 36 killed, 47 missing, and 100 seriously injured.

Almost all the food, medical supplies, and other stores were destroyed, over 80% of all housing and buildings knocked down, and all the military installations on the island were temporarily out of action. Over 60 planes were damaged as well, though most were repairable. Although new supplies had been brought to the island by this time, and emergency mess halls and sleeping quarters built for all hands, the scale of the damage was still very large. If the war had not ended on September 2, this damage, especially the grounding and damage to 107 amphibious craft (including the wrecking of four LSTs, two medium landing ships, a gunboat, and two infantry landing craft) would likely have seriously impacted the planned invasion of Japan (Operation Olympic).

In his *Report on the Surrender and Occupation of Japan* dated February 11, 1946, the Commander in Chief of the Pacific Fleet and Pacific Ocean Areas included an extract to give his own account of the October 9, 1945, storm, which was named *Typhoon Louise*. The full account of the storm is available as Serial 0395, World War II Command File, at the Operational Archives Branch of the Naval Historical Center in Washington, DC. A partial description of the storm is presented in the paragraphs that follow.

The typhoon developed on October 4, 1945, just north of Rota as a result of a barometric depression and the convergent flow of equatorial air and tropical air. Guam Weather Central called the storm of apparently weak intensity "Louise" and put out the first weather advisory on it at 041200Z, with further advisories following at intervals of six hours. Up to that time of the 16th advisory (080600Z), the storm was following a roughly predictable path to the NW and was expected to pass between Formosa and Okinawa and on into the East China Sea.

At this time, however, the storm began to veer sharply to the right and head north for Okinawa. The 17th advisory at 081200Z (081100I) showed this clearly, and units began to be alerted for the storm late in the evening of the 8th. The forecast for Okinawa was for winds of 60 knots, with 90 knot gusts in the early morning of 9 October, and passage of the center at 1030(I).

"Louise", however, failed to conform to pattern, and that evening, as it reached 25° N (directly south of Okinawa) it slowed to six knots and greatly increased in intensity. As a result, the storm, which struck in the afternoon of the 9th, has seldom been paralleled in fury and violence; the worst storm at Okinawa since the United States landings there in April, earlier in the year.

The sudden shift of the storm 12 hours before its expected maximum, from a predicted path 150 miles west of Okinawa to an actual path that brought the center of the storm less than 15 miles east of Okinawa's southeast coast, caught many craft in the supposedly safe shelter of Buckner Bay without time to put to sea far enough to clear the storm. The ninth of October found the Bay jammed with ships ranging in size from Victory ships to LCV(P)s. All units, both afloat and ashore, were hurriedly battening down and securing for the storm.

By 1000 the wind had risen to 40 knots, the barometer was down to 989 millibars, visibility was less than 800 yards, the seas were rising, and the rain was coming down in torrents, liberally mixed with salt spray. By 1200, visibility was zero, and the wind was 60 knots from the east and northeast, with tremendous seas breaking over the ships. Small craft were already being torn loose from their anchors, and larger ships were, with difficulty, holding by liberal use of their engines. At 1400 the wind had risen to 80 knots, with gusts of far greater intensity, the rain that drove in horizontally was more salt than fresh, and even the large ships were dragging anchor under the pounding of 30 to 35-foot seas.

The bay was now in almost total darkness and was a scene of utter confusion as ships suddenly loomed in the darkness, collided, or barely escaped colliding by skillful use of engines, and were as quickly separated by the heavy seas. Not all ships were lucky; hundreds were blown ashore, and frequently several were cast on the beach in one general mass of wreckage, while the crews worked desperately to maintain watertight integrity and to fasten a line to anything at hand in order to stop pounding. Many ships had to be abandoned. Sometimes the crews were taken aboard by other ships; more often they made their way ashore, where they spent a miserable night huddled in caves and fields. A few were lost.

By 1600 the typhoon reached its peak, with steady winds of 100 knots and frequent gusts of 120 knots. At this time the barometer dipped to 968.5 millibars. This was the lowest reading that the barometers recorded and was probably the point of passage of the center of the typhoon, but the maximum winds continued unabated for another two hours, the gusts becoming fiercer, if anything. During this period, the wind shifted to the north, and then to the northwest, and began to blow ships back off the west and north reefs of the Bay and across to the south, sometimes dragging anchor the entire way. These wild voyages by damaged ships caused a nightmare series of collisions and near escapes with other drifting ships and shattered hulks.

A typical experience was that of the Flagler (AK). Her anchors dragged at 1200, and despite the use of both engines she was blown ashore a mile north of Baten Ko by 1315, colliding with LST 826 on the way. Grounded, she began to pound, and all power was lost. At 1710, as the wind changed, FLAGLER was blown off the reef and back across the bay, grazed a capsized YF and then continued on with a 13° port list, no power, and the lower spaces and engine room beginning to flood. One anchor was lost, the other dragged across the bay. By 1800 she had moved two miles across the bay and had grounded on the east side of Baten Ko, alongside a DE hulk. Lines were made fast to the DE, but flooding continued, and AT 0545 ship was abandoned. A small party remained on board, however, and successfully stopped flooding as the typhoon subsided. FLAGLER was later salvaged.

Many other ships had similar stories. Southern Seas (PY) rammed or was rammed by five other ships, before sinking. Nestor (ARB) was forced to start maneuvering as early as 1020, in order to avoid Inca (IX), which had started to drag at 0950. In dodging Inca, Nestor slipped nearer to the beach, and was forced to put all engines ahead one third in order to hold position on her anchor. At 1230 Nestor again had to maneuver to narrowly avoid a collision with LST 826, which was dragging anchor very rapidly; but in so doing, Nestor nearly ran down ARD 27. Another LST, the 823, was being slowly driven towards Nestor. While maneuvering clear of 823, Nestor's anchor chain fouled the buoy to which an LCI was secured, and Nestor had to slip her anchor chain. Despite the full use of all engines, Nestor was being driven on shore by the increasing winds. The starboard anchor was let go but would not hold, and in clearing two more ships dragging anchor (ARD 22 and LCI 463), Nestor moved perilously close to the beach. At this time the winds were constantly rising, seas were breaking clear over the ship, and the conning tower was being deluged with saltwater and torrents of rain.

No sooner had the last two ships been cleared than YP 289 closed dead ahead, and it became necessary to back all engines to avoid a collision, but this put Nestor so close to the beach that she soon grounded. It was now 1345, only an hour and a quarter after first dodging LST 826. While grounded, Nestor was struck by YF 1079, was holed, and began to pound badly. At 1420 a sudden shift of wind drove Nestor off the beach, flipped her around end for end, and drove her back on the beach alongside Ocelot (IX 110). Breakers 20 to 30 feet high now pounded Nestor, flooding all starboard compartments aft of frame 25. At 1530 the wind again shifted, driving Nestor's stern against APL 14, completely crushing the stern, while the bow penetrated the side of Ocelot at frame 10. A few minutes later, Nestor settled in 24 feet of water. At 1945 all personnel and records were evacuated to APL 14.

Conditions on shore were no better. Twenty hours of torrential rain soaked everything, made quagmires of roads, and ruined virtually all stores. The hurricane winds destroyed from 50% to 95% of all tent camps and flooded the remainder. Damage to Quonset huts ran from 40% to 99% total destruction. Some of these Quonsets were lifted bodily and moved hundreds of feet; others were torn apart, galvanized iron sheets ripped off, wallboarding shredded, and curved supports torn apart. Driven from their housing, officers and men alike were compelled to take shelter in caves, old tombs, trenches, and ditches in the open fields, and even behind heavy road-building machinery, as the windswept tents, planks, and sections of galvanized iron through the air.

At the Naval Air Bases some 60 planes of all types were damaged, some of which had been tossed about unmercifully, but most of which were reparable. Installations suffered far more severely. The seas worked under many of the concrete ramps and broke them up into large and small pieces of rubble. All repair installations were either swept away or severely damaged. At Yonobaru, all 40' by 100' buildings were demolished, the same being true at the NATS terminal. Communication and meteorological services were blown out at most bases by 1900.

The storm center of typhoon "Louise" passed Buckner Bay at about 1600, from which time until 2000 it raged at peak strength. The storm was advancing at the rapid rate of 15 knots in a northerly, then northeasterly, direction, and by 2000 the center was 60 miles away. The winds gradually began to subside. Conditions in Buckner Bay were at this time somewhat improved by the wind's having veered to the northwest across the land mass of Okinawa, which reduced the size of the seas, and probably saved many more damaged ships from being driven off the reefs and sunk in deep water. Nevertheless, the subsidence at 2000 was a relative one, from "super-typhoon" to typhoon conditions, with steady winds of 80 and 60 knots throughout the night, and some gusts of higher velocity. All hands spent a wild, wet, night. Having left Okinawa, the storm proceeded NNE on a curving track. Ships of occupation groups anchored in Amami O Shima anchorage had a rough time, with winds over 70 knots; and Japan, from Nagasaki to Tokyo, was alerted for the storm. On the night of 10-11 October, "Louise" ran into cold air from over Japan and as a result the center of the typhoon occluded, moved aloft to the north, and eventually dissipated. Our forces from Nagasaki to Wakayama experienced winds of 40 to nearly 60 knots on the 11th and 12th. Ships at sea were enabled to maneuver clear of the worst of the storm, and sustained only minor damage, despite heavy seas.

This ended typhoon "Louise", but the damage it left behind on Okinawa was tremendous. Approximately 80% of all housing and buildings were destroyed or made unusable. Very little tentage was salvageable, and little was on hand as a result of previous storms. Food stocks were left for only 10 days. Medical facilities were so destroyed that an immediate request had to be made for a hospital ship to support the shore activities on the island. Casualties were low, considering the great numbers of people concerned and the extreme violence of the storm. This was very largely due to the active and well directed efforts of all hands in assisting one another, particularly in evacuation of grounded and sinking ships. By 18 October, reports had been sifted and it was found that there were 36 dead, 47 missing, and approximately 100 injuries, some of them serious.

The casualty list of ships was far greater, as detailed below. A total of 12 ships were sunk, 222 grounded, and 32 damaged beyond the ability of ships' companies to repair. ComServDiv 104 under Commodore T. J. Keliher, was assigned to the salvage work. By November 19, 79 ships had been refloated, and 132 were under repair. The remaining 53 badly damaged vessels still afloat had been, or were being, decommissioned, stripped, and abandoned. On November 14, ComServPac Vice Admiral W. W. Smith inspected the damage, and decided that only 10 ships were worth complete salvage, out of some 90 ships with major work to be done on them. This decision was made chiefly because similar types of ships were rapidly being decommissioned in the United States, and the cost of salvage would have been excessive for unneeded ships.

As it had at sea, repair work went on rapidly ashore as well. As a result of an earlier typhoon in September, extra stocks of food and tentage were already on the way from the United States to be stored on Okinawa. These were enroute on October 9, and in less than a week after the storm supplies had been built up, emergency mess halls and sleeping quarters had been erected for all hands, and 7500 men had been processed for return to the United States.

Over 55 years later, the men who were aboard LST-864 can well recall the terror of Typhoon Louise. They had no way of knowing at the time, however, just how serious it had been and exactly how much damage it had caused. For Allied and Japanese forces alike, the damage wrought by the storm was enormous. To clarify the danger the sailors were in, the Pacific Fleet Commander's Detailed Report of Typhoon Damage at Okinawa is presented in the pages that follow. No damage report was necessary, however, for those who lived through the storm to remember it for a lifetime!

DETAILED REPORT OF TYPHOON DAMAGE AT OKINAWA
(Based Upon Progress Reports to November 19, 1945)

AFD 13		Grounded - required tow to rear area for docking. Strip, abandonment. Decommissioned 11/24/45
AFD 14		Damaged - considered unsalvageable. Limited local repairs, for local use.
AFDL 32		Damaged - salvage doubtful. Strip, abandonment.
AK 156	ALAMOSA	Damaged - extent unknown
AK 181	FLAGLER	Refloated 10/29. Recommended return rear area and decommissioning
AMc 86		Grounded. Overturned. Flooded to main deck
AN 23	MAHOGANY	Refloated 10/23. Captain Black recommends tow to rear area.
AN 42	CLIFFROSE	Grounded
AN 52	SNOWBALL	Grounded. Beyond economical repair
AOG 4	WABASH	Damaged - extent unknown
AOG 25	CALAMUS	Refloated 10/24. Retain in service, repair
AOG 27	ESCATAWPA	Refloated 10/10/45
AOG 31	KANAWHA	Grounded. Refloated 10/19/45
AOG 40	SACANDAGA	Grounded. Strip, abandonment. Decommissioned 11/24/45
APA 68	BUTTE	Damaged - extent unknown
APC 19		Grounded.
APC 103		Grounded. Decommissioned 11/23/45.
APD 86	HOLLIS	Grounded. Not considered salvageable.
APD 36	GREENE	Grounded. Not considered salvageable. Decommissioned 11/24
APL 12		Refloated 10/25/45. Limited local repairs, for local use
APL 13		Grounded. Decommissioned 11/23/45.
APL 14		Grounded. Recommended for stripping.
APL 33		Refloated 11/24/45
ATF 117	WATERSEE	Sunk
ATF 115		Refloated 10/10/45
ARB 6	NESTOR	Grounded - recommended for decommissioning
ARB 7	SARPEDON	Damaged - extent unknown
ARV 3		
ARV 5		
ARG 9	MONA ISLAND	Refloated 10/15/45
ARS 16	EXTRICATE	Grounded - extent unknown
ATR 9		Damaged - extent unknown
ATR 191		Grounded

ARD 21		Grounded - salvage doubtful. Recover, tow to Guam, dock, refloated 11/20/45
ARD 22		Refloated 10/12/45
ARD 29		Refloated 10/12/45
ATA 177		Refloated 10/12/45
ATA 181		Grounded. Refloated 10/14/45
ATA 191		Grounded. Beyond economical salvage.
ATA 200		Refloated 10/12/45
Barge K-4058		Refloated 10/22/45
CM 12	WEEHAWKEN	Grounded. Not salvageable
DE 444	OBBERENDER	Refloated 11/3/45
DMS 2	LAMBERTON	Grounded
DMS 10	SOUTHARD	Grounded
DMS 17	DORSEY	Grounded
Dredge	MACKENZIE	Refloated 10/24/45
FS 406		Grounded
FS 409		Grounded
FS 411		Refloated 10/22/45
FS 552		Grounded
IX 91		Sunk
IX 110	OCELOT	Stripped, abandonment 10/29/45. Decommissioned
IX 163	CINNABAR	Stripped, abandonment 10/29/45. Decommissioned
IX 162	LIGNITE	Grounded
LCI 31		Grounded - Refloated 10/15/45. Captain Pohl recommends decommissioning and strip of all salvageable material
LCI 57		Grounded.
LCI 67		Grounded
LCI 73		Grounded - Refloated 10/14/45
LCI 127		Grounded.
LCI 230		Refloated 10/23/45
LCI 337		Grounded
LCI 339		Grounded
LCI 397		Grounded
LCI 399		Grounded
LCI 407		Damaged - extent unknown
LCI 410		Refloated 11/5/45
LCI 370		Refloated 11/7/45
LCI 463		Refloated 10/22/45
LCI 460		Refloated 10/12/45
LCI 470		Refloated 10/21/45
LCI 486		Grounded
LCI 550		Refloated 10/19/45
LCI 727		Refloated 10/21/45
LCI 728		Refloated 10/19/45
LCI 763		
LCI 796		
LCI 903		Grounded
LCI 992		Refloated 10/30/45
LCI 993		Damaged - extent unknown

LCI 678		Refloated 11/3/45
LCI 771		Grounded
LCI 1399		Damaged - extent unknown
LC(FF) 486		Grounded - strip, abandonment
LCS 4		Grounded - Refloated 10/19/45
LCS 69		Grounded
LCS 460		Grounded
LCS 550		Grounded
LCT 444		Refloated 10/19/45
LCT 507		Grounded
LCT 586		Grounded
LCT 763		Grounded
LCT 1231		Grounded
LCT 1261		Grounded
LCT 1276		Grounded
LCT 1330		Refloated 10/22/45
LCT 1382		Refloated 11/5/45
LCT 1420		Refloated 10/24/45
LSM 15		Sunk
LSM 9		Grounded
LSM 51		Grounded
LSM 79		Refloated 10/19/45
LSM 137		Grounded - strip, abandonment
LSM 141		Grounded
LSM 143		Grounded
LSM 170		Grounded
LSM 200		Grounded
LSM 273		Grounded
LSM 307		Grounded
LSM 334		Grounded - Refloated 10/11/45
LSM 356		Refloated 10/22/45
LSM 344		Grounded
LSM 361		Grounded
LSM 365		Grounded
LSM 406		Grounded
LSM 408		Grounded
LSM 437		Damaged - extent unknown
LSM 444		Grounded
LSM 458		Grounded
LSM 465		Grounded - refloated 10/14/45
LSM 468		Refloated 10/21/45
LSM 1120		Grounded
LST 169		Grounded
LST 494		Refloated 10/22/45
LST 501		Grounded
LST 534		Sunk
LST 561		
LST 568		Refloated 10/13/45
LST 675		Decommissioned

LST 684		Grounded
LST 690		Grounded
LST 717		Refloated 10/21 (CSD104 10/12)
LST 823		Grounded - Beyond economical salvage
LST 826		Grounded - Beyond economical salvage
LST 830		Grounded
LST 876		Grounded - Refloated 10/14/45
LST 890		Grounded - Refloated 10/19/45
LST 896		Grounded
LST 1001		Grounded - Refloated 10/1/45
LST 1128		Damaged - extent unknown
PB 37		Grounded
PC 584		Grounded - Beyond economical repair
PC 814		Grounded - Beyond economical repair
PC 590		Grounded - Beyond economical repair
PC 1018		Damaged
PC 1120		Grounded
PC 1128		Grounded - Beyond economical repair
PC 1178		Refloated 10/24/45. (CSD 104 refloated 10/16/45)
PC 1238		Refloated 10/19/45. Capsized. Heavily damaged. Decommissioned 11/23/45
PC 1239		Refloated 10/19/45
PC 1245		Refloated 10/19/45
PC 1418		Damaged - extent unknown. Beyond economical repair
PC 1419		Grounded
PC 1461		Grounded
PC 1126		Grounded - Decommissioned 11/23/45
PCS 1418		Grounded - Beyond economical salvage
PCS 1461		Grounded
PGM 27		Grounded - Beyond economical salvage
PGM 23		Refloated 10/21/45
PGM 1421		Grounded
PD 992		Refloated 11/7/45
PY	SOUTHERN SEAS	Sunk
SC 275		Grounded
SC 454		Grounded
SC 606		Grounded
SC 686		Grounded - Beyond economical repair
SC 716		Refloated 11/5/45
SC 727		Grounded - Beyond economical repair
SC 999		Grounded - Beyond economical repair. Decommissioned 11/23/45
SC 995		Grounded
SC 996		Grounded
SC 1012		Grounded - Deleted by Cincpac 132145
SC 1306		Grounded - Beyond economical repair
SC 1311		Damaged - extent unknown Refloated
SC 1314		
SC 1326		Grounded

SC 1328		Refloated 10/15/45
SC 1338		Refloated 10/24/45
SC 1368		Grounded
SC 1418		Grounded
SC 1461		Grounded
SC 1474		Refloated. Temporary repairs completed. Ready to proceed to U.S.
YMS 454		Grounded - Beyond economical salvage
YMS 90		Refloated 10/24/45. Return rear area, decommission
YMS 146		Grounded - Abandonment
YMS 148		Grounded
YMS 151		Grounded - Strip, abandonment
YMS 193		Refloated 11/6/45 (CSD 104 has refloated 10/45)
YMS 86		Damaged seriously but afloat
YMS 99		Refloated 11/2/45
YMS 193		Refloated 11/6/45
YMS 275		Grounded - Beyond economical repair. Strip, abandonment
YMS 292		Refloated 10/19/45
YMS 348		Grounded
YMS 381		Damaged - extent unknown
YMS 308		Refloated 11/6/45
YMS 383		Grounded - Sunk, strike from register
YMS 384		Sunk
YMS 424		Grounded - Beyond economical salvage
YMS 442		Refloated 10/19/45
YMS 590		Grounded
YSD 48		Sunk
YSD 64		Grounded
YSD 77		Damaged seriously but afloat
YF 552		Grounded
YF 606		Grounded - Refloated 11/20/45
YF 626		Grounded
YF 627		Grounded - Refloated 11/21/45
YF 718		Refloated 10/12/45
YF 731		Refloated 10/12/45
YF 739		Grounded - Recommended for stripping
YF 747		Refloated 10/22/45
YF 750		Grounded
YF 744		Refloated 10/24/45
YF 756		Damaged seriously but afloat
YF 757		Sunk
YF 739		Damaged - extent unknown. In service present location, then strip.
YF 442		Refloated 10/22/45
YF 292		Refloated 10/22/45
YF 993		Grounded
YF 1079		Grounded - Recommend for stripping
YO 111		Refloated 10/19/45
YO 112		Grounded
YO 122		Refloated 10/19/45

YOG 40		Grounded
YOG 75		Sunk, strip, abandonment
YOG 80		Refloated 11/20/45
YOGL 13		Grounded
YOGL 16		Grounded
YP 42		Grounded. Refloated 10/12/45
YP 235		Grounded
YP 236		Grounded
YP 239		Grounded - Recommended for stripping
YP 289		Sunk
YP 520		Grounded - Recommended striking from register
YP 529		Grounded
YP 620		Damaged - extent unknown
YTB 379	CANUCK	Sunk
YTB 386		Grounded
YTB 411		Sunk
YT 80		Grounded
YT 289		Grounded
YT 618		Refloated 11/5/45
YTL 422		Refloated 10/22/45
YTL 423		Refloated 10/24/45
YTL 550		Refloated 10/24/45
YTL 551		Grounded
YTL 552		Refloated 10/21/45
YDG 6		Damaged seriously afloat
YNG 28		Damaged - extent unknown
SS MONROE VICTORY (XAK)		Grounded.
SS JACK SINGER		Grounded.
SS WILLIAM RALSTON		Grounded.
SS RICHARD J. OGLESBY		Grounded.
SS HARRINGTON EMERSON		Refloated 10/27/45
SS JOSEPH E. JOHNSTON		Grounded
SS OVID BUTLER		Refloated 10/12/45
SS BROCK-HOLST LIVINGSTON		Damaged seriously but afloat
SS AUGUSTINE HEARD		Damaged - extent unknown
SS GUTZON BORGLUM		Damaged - extent unknown

SS DAVID S. BARRY		Damaged - extent unknown
SS FRANCIS WILSON		Damaged - extent unknown
SS JOHN M. MILLER		Damaged - extent unknown
SS EDGAR W. NYE		Damaged - extent unknown
SS JOSEPH HOLT		Refloated 10/18/45

****

WORK CREW ON DECK, NAMES UNKNOWN

Jerry D. Crutchfield

Hubert "Buzzard" Tinlin

Ralph Thompson

Sylvester Szerzinski

John Scott

Clyde Smith

Earl E. Sandage

Richard Claude Rose (or Ross)

Leonard Walczak

James M. Ferrell

Harold Gene Bittaker

Walter E. Thomas

Carlo M. Jacobson

Charles (or Harley) Adams

William K. Warren

D. L. Wever

Charles Grandt Winters

Arthur Joseph Guida

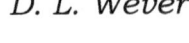

THE LADY LUCK

Wilbur Brandmair

Herbert Benjamin Myers

Norman Call May

Joe Alexander Terry

Garland Harold Leverett

Christopher R. Regal

Byron Francis O'Brien

Issac Newton Pitts

CHAPTER 6

HISTORY OF THE U.S.S. LST-864

The record provided by the *Dictionary of American Fighting Ships* states that the USS LST-864 was laid down on October 3, 1944, at Jeffersonville, Indiana, by the Jeffersonville Boat and Machine Company. It was launched on November 18, 1944, sponsored by Mrs. Viola J. Wathen. The ship was commissioned on December 13, 1944, for active military service in the Pacific Theater of the conflict against Japan during World War II.

LST-864 was a 327-foot "Landing Ship/Tank," one of around 100 identical vessels built by the well-known "Jeffboat" facility during the peak armament construction year of 1944. Approximately one of the 2000-ton hulls splashed into the waters of the Ohio River every three days. All together, a total of 1,051 of these ships were built at various facilities during WW II. The LSTs become one of the greatest offensive weapons of United States in the war, and many consider its contributions to be on par with those of the cruisers, the battleships, and the destroyers.

During the war, LST-864 was assigned to the Asiatic-Pacific Theater and participated in the assault and occupation of Okinawa Gunto from April through June of 1945. Following the war, she performed occupation duty in the Far East and saw service in China until mid-January of 1947. She returned to the United States and was decommissioned on May 1 of 1947 and struck from the Navy list on May 22 of that same year. On June 26, 1948, the ship was sold to Consolidated Builders, Inc., of Seattle, Washington, and subsequently scrapped. When the war ended, some LSTs remained in service but most were either scrapped, modified, or given to Navies of other countries. Some remained in service and saw action in Korea, Viet Nam, and even in the Cuban Blockade.

LST-864 received one battle star for World War II service. The purpose of this book is to take a retroactive look at the missions assigned to the ship and to recognize the contribution of the officers and crewmen that manned her. Had they not helped to win the war for the Allied forces, Japan might still rule or otherwise dominate Manchuria, Korea, China, the Philippines, and other parts of the world today--all countries they have attacked during World War II or at other times in recent history. In this instance, most careful examiners have concluded that this was indeed a "good war," one that reversed armed aggression that had already taken place and prevented the occurrence of even further aggression. Those who performed military service during this period are fully deserving of National respect and gratitude.

The following paragraphs contain the ship's history as recalled by her captain, Richard W. Wathen:

```
              U.S.S. L.S.T. 864
              FLEET POST OFFICE
              SAN FRANCISCO, CAL.

                 SHIP'S HISTORY

     Winter had definitely set in when LST-864 slid into the
muddy Ohio at Jeff Boat Company of Jeffersonville, Indiana,
on December 2, 1944. Snow had not yet fallen but it
promised to arrive soon on the cold and gusty wind that
whipped down the river from the North. The crew spent most
of it's time below decks but there was plenty to do and
thousands of spare parts to be inventoried. The
compartmentation proved confusing at first, even on an LST,
and more than one hand found himself in the shaft alley when
he wanted the engine room. One deck hand fell asleep in the
back of the issue room and was reported as two days AWOL
before anyone discovered him.

     The Ohio wound and curved its way to Cairo, Illinois,
where it joined with Old Father of Waters to flow Gulfward.
Although somewhat wider from that point on the Mississippi
still held many a sand bar or submerged log and all hands
agreed as to the skill of the river pilots who guided the
ship without the aid of the wheel using only the automatic
steering lever.

     By the end of the first five days some of the newness
had worn off when the lights of Memphis hove into view
everyone was eager to go ashore. What made it tougher than
ever was anchoring almost within hailing distance of the
brightly lighted city and prohibiting anyone to leave the
ship. So the liberty hounds grumbled and growled and went
below in a huff vowing they would get even in New Orleans.
```

From the moment 864 hit the pier in the City of the Mardi Gras until she finally shoved off, her hull and innards were a hum of activity. Navy shipfitters swarmed aboard like bees and the mast was rigged in a jiffy. They built ways on the main deck for an LCT. We loaded more supplies, we inventoried them as they came aboard.

Inspectors were a dime a dozen. Each piece of equipment and machinery was checked and then checked again. To a man who had just returned by 0800 from an extraordinarily hard liberty this never-ending checking proved a nightmare. In spite of what lay ahead many a sigh of relief was audible the day we shoved off for St. Andrews Bay, Florida, for shakedown.

When it was over about ten days later and the ship traveled back to New Orleans both the crew and Officers felt they knew the score 100% better then, than two weeks previous. A signalman probably expressed the general sentiment of the crew when he said that outside of the sleepless nights spent scrubbing bulkheads, shakedown was "kind of fun".

Thirteen days later on January 13th, the 864 had acquired LCT 1428 squatting on the main deck and a tank deck full of radar and radio parts destination Balboa, Canal Zone. Early the same morning she left the river's mouth and moved out on the Gulf.

The five day trip to Coco Solo proved an unforeseen ordeal, especially the last two days when the Caribbean Sea acted up and threatened the ship to its first rough weather. What a relief to steam into the quiet lagoon at Cristobal, C. Z., and tie up at Coco Solo. But the Engineers had no sooner left the engine rooms than back they went to warm the mains for we were ordered through the Canal at once.

The great Gatun locks dwarfed such a small ship and soon had her afloat on Gatu Lake, far above the Atlantic. By this time it was late afternoon and we had only reached the cut leading to Miraflores Locks before darkness set in. Our newly installed phonograph was ready for operation and while the ship floated lazily along under the full moon everyone gathered topside to listen to the strains of music. One of the records, "Waiting for the Robert E. Lee," inspired the Negro line handlers on the shore and they treated everyone to some old-fashioned and fancy stepping.

We lay at Balboa for five days discharging the cargo at a slow rate because we were unable to beach and the whole tank deck was unloaded through the cargo hatch. Sailing was delayed an additional day by a load of radio parts for San Diego, but it was only a third of the previous load and left room for an occasional game of basketball.

Late in the afternoon all lines were cast off and we moved into an ocean which we were to see a lot of. The broad Pacific. But except for a two-day sortie through the Gulf of Tehauntepec she lived up to her name and lay like glass on all sides. The LCT was crowded in the afternoons with sunbathers.

San Piego proved a relief' from Balboa in that the Spanish dictionary could be discarded, but it might have been traded for shoulder pads when strolling the sidewalk. The city ran a close second to Norfolk for the title "BeeHive". But even so, our ten days stay ended ten days too soon and we shoved off for Port Hueneme, 10 hours journey to the North, with reluctance.

SeeBees made their headquarters at this desolate camp where they worked on us for about 8 hours and decorated each side with a double row of steel pontoons. This pulled the ship way down in the water and made her handle sluggishly but it minimized our roll, a fact for which we were most glad three days later when we encountered the roughest see yet off the Oregon Coast which lasted until we entered the peaceful and beautiful strait of Juan de Fuca leading into Seattle.

Seattle was a busy place, but a great liberty town. It was last stop for State-side supplies and requisitions flew like mad. Trips were made to Bremerton in search of salvaged parts and every returning liberty party raised the waterline an inch with magazines, food, knick-knacks and gadgets.

The third day there we proceeded to Lake Washington and loaded the 1903rd Aviation Engineers on board. We lay off Port Orchard until ready for sea and proceeded out in company with seven other LST's under command of Commander J. H. Motes aboard the LST-854.

Nobody paid much attention to the retracting shore-line but since then many have wished they had taken the time to memorize every detail.

Next stop--Pearl Harbor, after a twelve day trip full of flag hoist drills and shipboard emergency practice. General Quarters sounded every morning and night and sometimes during the day. We had fires on the bow, the fantail, the tank deck, the main deck, and every possible spot except the mast. But when we got through, there was no emergency that couldn't be handled.

Pearl was worse than Norfolk for being crowded because there, one couldn't jump into a car and get away from it all.

The Navy Yard was the busiest place on the face of the earth. We were glad to leave but cursed ourselves for that very gladness a few short months later.

We held true to our habit of leaving port on the 13th of the month at Pearl Harbor, for on March 13th, we pointed the bow at the Marshalls and commenced making 270 turns. Eleven days later on the 24th we dropped anchor in the most desolate anchorage, from the viewpoint of the crew, of any in the entire Pacific. Eniwetok hasn't much to offer, that we all agreed.

Guam followed and then Ulithi, in that order. On the day before we were to arrive at Ulithi, word reached us that the Randolph had been bombed in that very harbor. It was the closest we had yet been to the war and everyone felt the incident acutely. But only blue alerts characterized our stay in that tremendous lagoon, besides, of course, liberties on Mog-Mog. We knew blue alerts would not long be the most exciting event on April 11th, for on that day, we steamed out, still under the command of Commander Motes, for Okinawa and IE Shima. For the first time we were accompanied by escorts.

On the 18th, we arrived at Okinawa and anchored in Nago Wan off the upper Easter Coast of the Island. That night came our first flash red, control yellow, and we made smoke for a solid hour. No planes came our way but we knew action was hot and heavy off Hagushi to the south, where heavy units of the Fleet lay. The anti-aircraft tracers were plainly visible.

Word to proceed to IE Shima and disembark the combat Engineers was received on April 20th. That night and the following, as we layoff IE watching the fighting thru glasses, our sleep was interrupted by frequent calls to

General Quarters, but for some reason the Japanese left our area alone and we saw no planes. The action was still centered around Hagushi for we could see the firing.

Commander Anderson and Commander Motes took charge of the ship; and directed her thru the treacherous reefs and onto the beach at 1545 on April 22nd. The vehicles rolled directly onto the pontoons thence to the sandy beach. Work progressed without let up, but that night sniper shots struck the pontoons which we had slung along side and were reported by the signalman to have ricocheted off the conn. We went to Gen. Quarters because of air alerts as usual.

Loading was completed at 0700 the following morning and 1445 found us at Hagushi awaiting orders relating to the pontoons. At 1400 we did so. Again that night Nago Nan, we strained our eyes for enemy planes but saw none.

On April 26th, we launched LCT-1428 and her crew, which had been aboard since New Orleans, left for good. The clear main deck seemed too good to be true but it was well that it was so for beginning that night and for the succeeding three, we ran to General Quarters every hour during the night.

Our 46 gun fired at a Bogie on the first night scored no hits. On the second night, Jap "Bettys" came over in force to bomb the Okinawa Airstrips, Kadon and Yenton, near Hagushi. Although covered by smoke every ship in the harbor fire at the planes, no matter what the range. Smaller craft and even boats with smokepots pinged away with 30 caliber shells that whistled dangerously near the conn.

Thru an opening in the smoke, we observed a "Betty" within range at 0245. All guns opened fire but she was soon out of range although the searchlights kept her in their beams. While all hands had their eyes on the plane off the bow a Kamikazi sneaked in low from seaward, but some ship, evidently one of the destroyers ashore off our fantail, caught her with a burst and the first we saw of her was a great burst of flame. She sailed in but was unable to crash any ship and ended with a great splash in the water off our starboard quarter.

The next, night was merely a repetition but no planes approached so close although we joined in heavy fire on two Japanese ships engaged in bombing the airstrip. The following morning, at 0800, April 29th, we joined in convey, again under Command of Commander J. H. Motes, and headed back to Ulithi for voyage repairs.

- - - - - - - - - -

Life for the next month and a half seemed somewhat dull after the excitement of Okinawa and IE Shima. We remained for a while at Ulithi, from there a step Eastward to Leyte where we anchored for about a month before beaching at Tolosa for equipment and men of the 872nd Aviation engineer's Battalion, Company "C".

This trip up to Okinawa was under the command of Commander A. E. Anderson of the Coast Guard, who had supervised our beaching at IE Shima two months previous for it was now June12th.

Hagushi was somewhat different this time we anchored there for the number of Japanese aircraft which managed to infiltrate the cordon of American night fighters was considerable fewer. Also, the ships at anchor were under strict orders not to fire but to blanket themselves in heavy smoke. During the entire time we were at Okinawa not a shot was fired from the ship in spite of sighting Jap planes thru the thin haze overhead.

Upon unloading on Orange Beach Number 2, we proceeded to Saipan for logisitics repairs unde the tactical command of Captain J. S. Laidlaw USN who accompanied the convoy on LCFF 1080.

At Saipan, we played lots of basketball being undefeated in abut 20 games which included an aircraft carrier and two at GC's. On the last day of June we dry-docked for work on the screws and bottom. The word which we had dreamed of was received on July 21st. Yes, orders to Pearl, from there we could only hope. In the company of 5 other LSTs, we began the 19 day journey. The Second day out the LST-476 dropped out due to engine trouble. At 1500 on the following day, LST-1002 received orders to return. Where there had been six there were now four. We began to eye one another suspiciously as if to say, "Who's nest, Buddy? Let's hope it's you and not me!"

But the remaining four continued all the way and early on August 5th, we arrived at Pearl and proceeded to West Loch. The Captain immediately went ashore for further word while we waited both for that and our long absent mail.

While at Pearl, came the end of the war, the most precious word we had ever received, and we felt that "Frisco was a sure thing". The Navy felt otherwise, however, and on August 20th, we moved down West Loch to Iroquois Point where we loaded Naval Mobile Communications Unit #460.

We were to proceed to Eniwetok and Guam and thence to Tokyo Bay, but early on August 26th, we received a message routing us to Midway Island. Supposedly the first LST there, we picked up PC 602 as escort and together we sailed west again, right into Tokyo Bay and anchored off Yokosuka Naval Base surrounded by the greatest array of Naval Power ever witnessed, part of the combined forces of the American and Allied Fleets.

The Unit was unloaded on September 10th, after which we moved to inner harbor, where we moored awaiting orders. They came on the 27th when we moved out alone enroute to Leyte Gulf again. The following day and night were the roughest encountered by the 864 for we rolled and tossed in the highest sea we had yet seen. Word was later received that we had hit the
"Tail-end" of a typhoon. All hands agreed that if it was the "Tail-end," they fervently wished they might never encounter the center.

Leyte had nothing or us, not even much mail, so after being there for week we proceeded to Subic Bay, or so we thought, but again were detoured enroute and made Lingayen Gulf our next stop instead.

At the conclusion of Ship's History, we intercepted a message ordering us to beach at Agoo, to load a Quartermaster Unit of the 6th Army and proceed to Sasebo Naval Base on Kyushu, Japan.

* * * * *

Crewmen – Second Crew: Richard Phillips, Bill Reed and Salvador Martinez aboard LST-864 in route to China.

Okinawa, in the South China Sea, was the site of the bloodiest Pacific battle. The American death toll was 12,500 killed and 36,000 wounded; the Japanese death toll was 187,000.

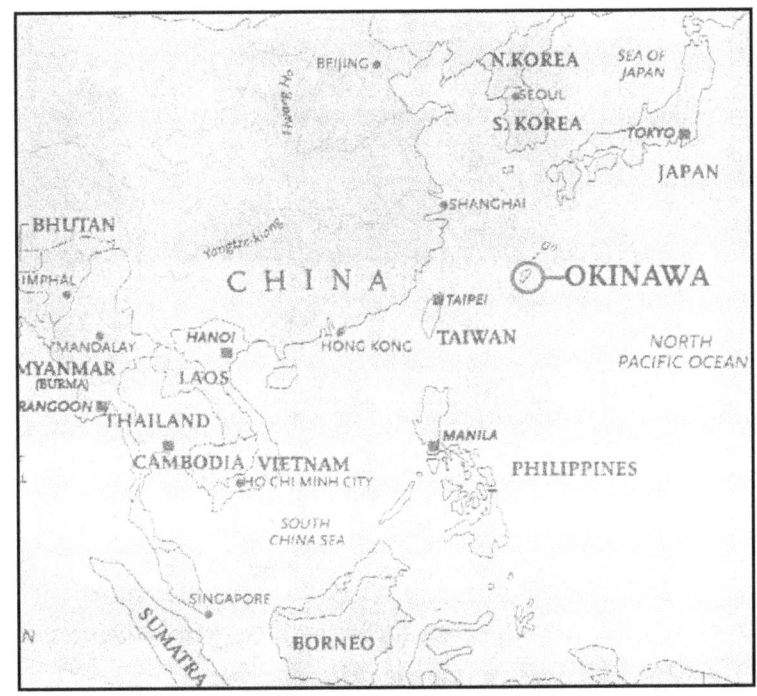

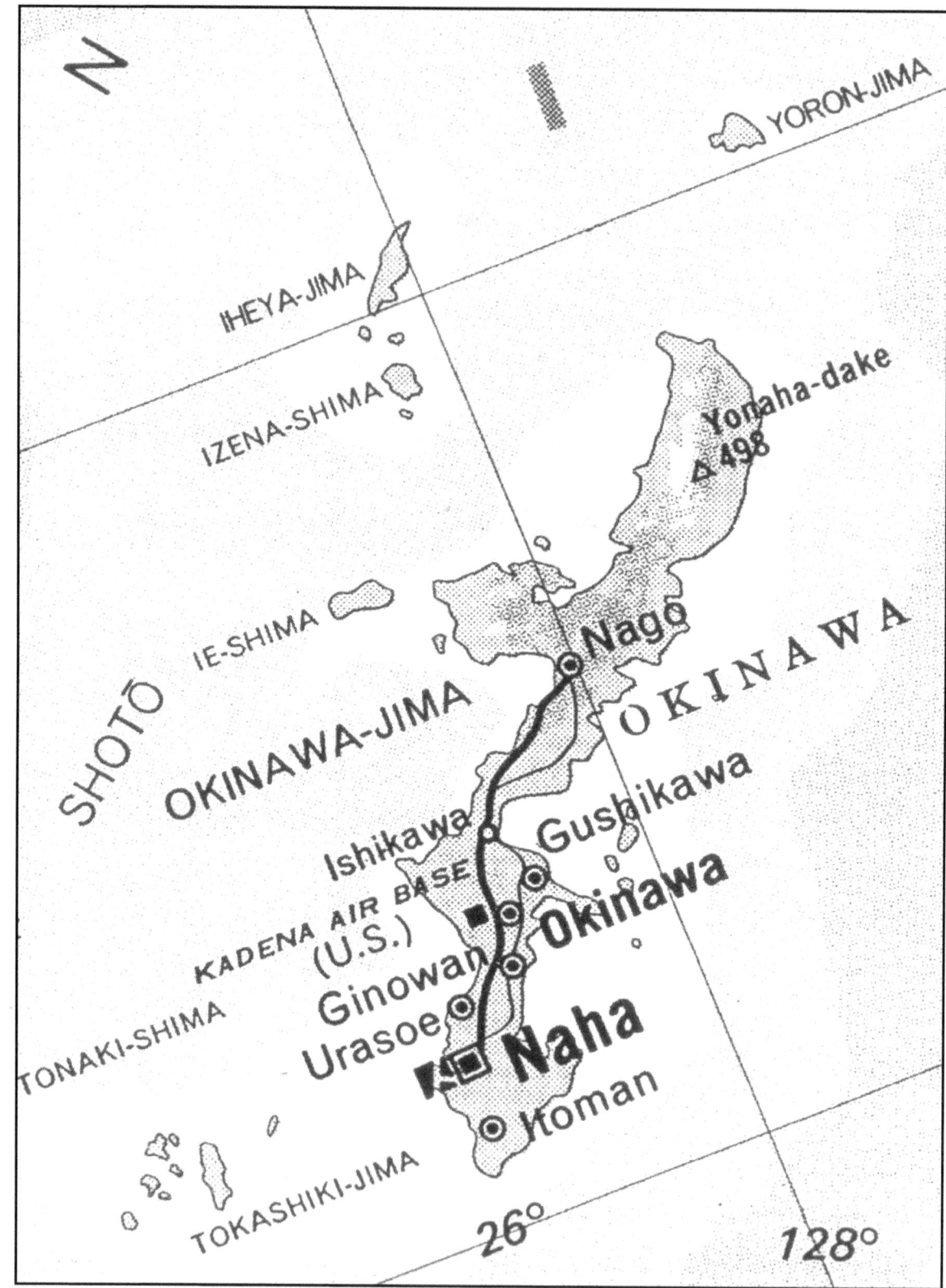

OKINAWA. 187,000 Japanese died in the invasion of Okinawa, 93,000 troops and 94,000 civilians. Many of the civilians died by committing suicide.

Road work at Okinawa

Sailors on leave. Andy DiPalma (top right); others unnamed

Andy DiPalma (right) and an unnamed crewman

The USS LST-864, in San Francisco

Crewmen Robert Martin (left), "Little Brown," and unnamed

CHAPTER 7

WARTIME MEMORIES OF CAPTAIN RICHARD B. WATHEN

Richard B. "Dick" Wathen, the first commanding of the USS LST-864, was a man of many accomplishments when he died in March 19, 2001, at the age of 83. Born in Jeffersonville, Indiana, he graduated from Princeton University and the School of Law at Indiana University before joining the Navy during World War II.

The ship he served on during the war, The USS LST-864, was built and launched on December 7, 1944, at the "Jeffboat and Machine Company, Inc." facility in his own hometown. After being christened by his own wife, Amelie (Walmsley) Wathen, it was taken down the Ohio River to New Orleans to join the war effort.

As a skipper, Wathen served in the thick of things in the Pacific Theater of the war against Japan. By the time the war was over, the ship had played a significant part in the conflict, seeing action at Okinawa, the Philippines and China. Following the war, she made two trips to Japan.

When the war was over, he was employed for four years as a CIA agent in Europe before returning to Jeffersonville launch a career as an attorney. This turned out to be another career move that went well for him.

Later, he successfully campaigned for and won a political office, representative of 71st District in the Indiana State legislature, which includes much of Clark County in that state. In this capacity, he served the residents of Jeffersonville and Southern Indiana for a total of 19 years.

Highly thought of when he retired from the legislature in 1990 at the age of 73, Wathen had a reputation for cooperative effort rather than political partisanship. He is recalled as a grass-roots campaigner who called or visited voters personally, one who always had a pool of friends willing to campaign for him.

When he retired from the House, he donated 3.5 acres of his family's riverfront property to the city as a thank-you gift to the constituents who had elected him time and again. His service to community and country are commemorated by a public park that was build by the City of Jeffersonville on the land he donated. The park was named Duffy's Landing in memory of his mother, at his request. Duffy was his mother's maiden name.

In addition to his major career achievements, Wathen was also proud of two additional personal accomplishments. First, he helped to the Clark Maritime Centre in Jeffersonville, Indiana. Second, he wrote two books, one a non-fiction account about his time in political office (called *"Wathen's Law"*) and the other a book of non-fiction (called *"The Only Yankee"*). Both were published by Regnery Publishing, Inc., of Chicago, Illinois.

Today, Richard B. "Dick" Wathen is buried in Jeffersonville, Indiana, his hometown, right where he always wanted to be. He spent most of his life in the service of his fellow citizens and his country, and he never forgot the men he served with during World War II on the USS LST-864, *The Lady Luck*. Before his death, he wrote memoirs to document his military experience, a record that was distributed at the first LST-864 Reunion in 1996. A portion of that handout appears in the pages that follow. A list of LSTs damaged or destroyed is included at the end the chapter, just to show what fate the crew might have met during the war had they not had the good fortune of serving aboard *"The Lady Luck."*

OFFICERS AND CREWMEN ON DECK

Captain's view of the stern of the ship while at sea.

" MEMORIES . . . "

By: Richard B. Wathen
January, 1991

INTRODUCTION

<u>DECEMBER 7, 1944</u>

LST 864 departed from the yards of Jeffboat on December 7, 1944. Our 327-foot Landing Ship Tank was one of some 100 identical ships built by Jeffboat during the peak construction year of 1944. This would figure to about one huge 2000-ton hull going sideways with a splash into the Ohio River every three days. Let us never forget the contribution made by Jeffboat to the war effort. The LST became one of the great offensive weapons of the United States. It was on a par with the battleship, the cruiser and the destroyer in bringing victory over what I still think of as the forces of evil in the modern world.

As a Navy Lieutenant, age 27, with slightly more than two years combat experience, I was the skipper of LST 864. Although we did not have a formal name the crew rather early on gave the ship their own nickname--we called her Lady Luck.

With a crew of 100 men and 10 officers, and only five of us who had ever been to sea, I suppose the nickname Lady Luck was well chosen. The fact that a bunch of greenhorns like us could navigate a huge creation of welded steel plate through the Panama Canal and across the broad Pacific to Okinawa seems as I think back, a kind of miracle.

Going down river to New Orleans we made one stop at Memphis, where we swung at anchor with the lights of the city only a few hundred yards away. We sailors were dying to go ashore and see something of the night life in what seemed like one of the most exciting cities in the world. But no one was allowed to leave the ship. We were under the discipline of the special pilot crew that was responsible for getting us safely to New Orleans.

At New Orleans some finishing work was done, which

included the mounting of two 40-millimeter guns on the bow and stern, with five 20-millimeter Oerlikens mounted on each side of the ship. We did go on a shakedown cruise for a few days to Panama City, Florida, where we made landings under simulated battle conditions. Just as important as the landing was the procedure of retraction, which was accomplished through the use of a stern anchor, which was heaved in at the same time as our twin diesels engines were put in full speed reverse.

Returning to New Orleans we spent six final days in the Crescent City, making our final departure on the cold gray morning on January 16.

My wife had come to New Orleans to spend Christmas and New Years. Our parting and farewell at the Pontachatrain Hotel was a sad moment. We were to be apart for a full year, not nearly so long as many other young couples, but it did seem like an eternity, especially when added on to my two years of duty in the Atlantic and Mediterranean.

My personal diary includes an account of the voyage of LST 864 through the Panama Canal and up the West Coast to San Diego and eventually to Seattle where we loaded a company of Army Aviation Engineers for the invasion of Okinawa. In this condensed version I have skipped the account of our passage to Pearl Harbor, Guam and the Marshall Islands, starting the narration on April 17, 1945 just as we were approaching the coast of Okinawa.

TUESDAY, APRIL 17, 1945

The sea is calm today, disturbed only by small ripples like a pond. There is no swell. All seems peaceful and quiet. The air is still, and yet less than 200 miles away one of the fiercest battles of the Pacific is raging at Okinawa.

I will be glad to see our men and supplies off loaded, not that I am tired of our passengers but I am anxious to deliver the military goods, human and otherwise, that we have been carrying such a distance that I grow tense with the passage of each day. They came on board at Seattle on February 26. A fine looking husky lot of men. When there was a delay in the embarkation one of them yelled out, "Get these men out of this hot sun." In Seattle that morning 53 days before it was cold and drizzling, a light rain.

But with our landing a matter of hours away the Army is getting nervous in the service too, most of them never having had duty of any kind overseas, let alone fighting in a war.

Doubtless we all have a touch of buck fever.

WEDNESDAY, APRIL 18

Over the short range radio we can hear the salvoes of guns being fired, opening with the call names of cruisers and battleships. We are almost in the thick of it. I am glad that I lost at cards the past two nights. I want to save all my luck, my good luck.

Today is the day we have been waiting for. Needless to say there was no desire for late sleeping. I got up at 0400 for a course change and did not turn in again. On the shore of Okinawa we could see the flash of star shells and hear the rumble of field pieces and then see the glare of the explosion. This was the real thing.

At 0800 the convoy split up and we LSTS, some 10 of us, went on our way alone. Our first real sight of land was a small island on our port side. Reminded me of the Azores, half way around the world from us, although it looked more rugged. The fields were cultivated in neat plots right up to the top of the hilly terrain. There was a small village down below. I could not see a soul on the island this morning.

In about two hours we steamed past Naha Harbor. We could see hundreds of ships and three battleships pouring shells from their big guns into the town. When the shells detonated you could see a big flash, then there would be a concussion that would shake our small ship with a thud. We steamed on for several hours more to Naga Wan Harbor. As we filed in a cruiser, the Biloxi, was lobbing broadsides over a hill with an observation plane spotting high above.

As we drew near the anchorage we could see smoke in all the hills and hear the tremendous concussion of some kind of mortar. This was the real McCoy.

On the beach we could see much equipment, much confusion. Our soldiers who were all keyed up at the idea of being on their own on the beach must remain aboard not knowing their fate. In a sense an anticlimax, but an exciting one. Gone is the oppressive feeling of fatigue and weariness that experienced last night. Everyone is keyed up, alert and excited. No one seems to give fear a thought. American youth an inspiring lot.

THURSDAY, APRIL 19

I was summoned to the Flag today for a skipper's conference. We were told that we would hit the beach at Ie Shima, six of us would leave today and two tomorrow. Something definite at last. I returned to the ship, then gave the crew a briefing over the PA system. A storm blew up in the afternoon, apparently delaying departure of the first six ships, so the delay continues. Anyway we know the big day is about to begin. And this trying business of waiting, waiting completely in the dark as to future events is about over. This business has been long and hard for all of us.

Excitement keeps one pretty well keyed up and the time passes quickly. We learn that Ernie Pyle was killed today close by on Ie Shima, which brings the danger home to all of us. We hear the big drive is on at Okinawa and the rumbling of guns all day long and the flares during the night give proof.

The army got their mail today ruining a screw on the LCVP in the process. Anyway, that is one thing we don't have to bother with. Tomorrow will be a large day so I am turning in.

FRIDAY, APRIL 20

We were receiving messages from midnight to 0400 telling us to get underway to shift anchorage. Then at 0430 over the radio came condition red flash yellow--signifying an air alert and ordering us to fire at anything. We went to General Quarters and our smoke machines put out quantities of protective smoke.

Finally we secured and I turned in for two blissful hours. Up at 0700. Bound and determined to get some souvenirs, so in we went in the small boat to the Town of Naha. Quite a thrill setting feet on Japanese soil. This is a beautiful place. The houses about half thatched roofs and half red tile. Some had no floors, others a rough wooden planking for, floors. Back to the ship and after lunch I lay down to take a nap. In 15 minutes we had orders to raise anchor. On the wayout we nearly smashed into an LST that had its anchor ball flying but was moving ahead testing engines. Don't know how we missed him. I backed down full and we stopped short a hair.

In an hour we were standing off Ie Shima. Very trying. From 1500 to 1700 we lay to. While eating dinner we got the order to get under way. We steamed away from the island, but only to make the Japs think we were leaving. Then coming in again this time to anchor, the Japs started firing at us. I saw a shell splash about 100 yards beyond us and explode. Pretty exciting. When we anchored we all made smoke which was thick as soup. Me a peaceful home loving citizen in the midst of all this shell fire and smoke, planes and war. Quite a thing.

SUNDAY, APRIL 22

Up early, 0400. Urgent that we get an order to make our landing. We have been ready, all morning. At 1000 when nothing happened and we got a message to the effect that we would unload by pontoon I went over to LCI 785, which seemed to have something to do with ordering ships into the beach. On board was an army captain, one of the best examples of operational fatigue I have ever seen. He had a bunch of golf tees stuck in a board full of holes, each tee representing a ship and its position. I could tell at a glance that his little board was inaccurate, so I set him straight on the whereabouts of our ship. Then he smiled at me queerly and said, "This board takes the place of my brain." That startled me. Sane or insane I persuaded him to send us in next, taking the place of LST 957 and letting her have the more difficult job of unloading by pontoon. Back aboard our ship they were showing the movie, Destroyer. At the most exciting part we got a message. "Prepare to move in." In a flash Commander Motes was on board and with a minimum of delay our hull was grading against the rocky beach.

We all flocked ashore. One of the first things we did was to gawk at an old Jap civilian who had surrendered. A quaint little man like a dwarf he seemed perfectly at home in his surroundings on the beach with American servicemen all around him.

As the unloading progressed, and when the tons of equipment and rolling stock came out of the open bow of our ship. I felt like thanking the Lord who had brought us all the way from Jeffersonville, Indiana.
Tomorrow is another day and what it brings we don't know, but have delivered the goods across 7600 miles of ocean.

APRIL 23

As directed we left Ie Shima at 1330 and proceeded to Hagushi, 11 miles away.

So far we have carried 600 tons cargo 1600 miles, our first load, New Orleans to Balboa. Also 100 officers and men

1600 miles.

Then from Seattle to Okinawa 200 troops 7600 miles, taking 54 days. Cargo 700 tons.

We still carry the LCT on our fore deck, 200 tons, and the pontoon causeways on each side, 100 tons.

Now that we are beginning to hit our stride this duty is starting to be fun. The last 36 hours have been grueling but exciting. Now I can understand the remarks a man made yesterday who had been in a number of amphibious operations. He referred to one operation as a dull operation, to another as an interesting invasion. He had become like so many of us, a connoisseur of invasions, a war dilettante.

Some of our men and officers have changed their ways of thinking about war. While we were on the beach at Ie Shima a number of them strayed around the nearby fields.

They saw women and children rotting in heaps. They saw a dead mother holding a dead child to her breast. In the hand not supporting the child she clutched a grenade.

I was about four feet from a Jap civilian in a jeep. He had come down from the hills to surrender: The civilians fight because they have been told we will murder their men and rape their women. Those of them that we are feeding are changing their minds. But it seems to me they will bear hatred for years to come because of the number of women and children we have had to kill. That doesn't bother me much.

This little old man I looked at was a queer sort of midget. He looked to me more like a Chinese with his black whiskers three or four inches long, and the black sparkling eyes. He was dirty and wounded in the leg, but as I say did not seem discontented with his lot.

FRIDAY, APRIL 25

Last night was the night of the full moon and we were all set for a long hard night with the Japs. We were given a flash red control green that lasted only a few minutes. Other than this interruption at 0230 I had the best night's sleep in a long while and awoke refreshed.

The port director asked us if we were in all respects RFS--ready for sea. So I suppose we will be hitting the trail soon.

I felt tired and stale last night after launching the LCT from our fore deck. It was the lowest I have felt in sometime. I was homesick and wanted to go home. That was all there was to it. I wanted my soft little wife to cuddle up against me.

Launching the LCT was quite a sight. We had carried the thing 10,000 miles from New Orleans and were well tired of it and the crew. There were considerable preparations to be made in clearing a path for the ugly duckling, such as clearing the remaining guns and life rails. Then too it was necessary to put an 11 degree list to starboard, so she would slide down the ways. All that figured ahead of time. We managed a 10 degree list by filling all starboard ballast tanks but to save our necks we could not get more than 10 degrees so we let it go at that. We cut her loose and down the great wooden ways she went, 200 tons and more than 100 feet long. She hit the water with a terrific splash, righted her self and all was well. A tremendous relief to me, for there was $200,000 in equipment that I had been lugging around for four months and it would have been tragic to have lost it.

Jack Holland, our first lieutenant, did a fine job. He is a tremendously capable, energetic and talented boy, he has drive and ability. I believe the world will hear from him some day.

SATURDAY, APRIL 26

Last night and the night before were busy. In the afternoon of the 27th we received a radio message warning us of suicide attacks and air attacks in general. That night they came. First they attacked the shore and dropped their eggs around the air field. There were bright flares and flames but I did not hear of much damage that resulted.

Shortly afterward, fire from the shore began streaming out toward us in white bursts of tracers. We were not hit so apparently we were out of range. In a few minutes the big thrill came. A Jap plane was caught in the cross of two giant searchlights. A medium range bomber. All of us opened fire and the bay was lit with tracers. But the plane seemed to be out of range.

In a few minutes we fired on another plane caught by the searchlights. About an hour later we had the biggest thrill. A kamikaze plane attempted to sneak in among the convoy in the opposite direction from the first plane. A ship's gun caught him and he went streaming down in the water in a burst of flame.

Learned the next day that there must have been a considerable number of planes we did not see. One C3 was sunk by a suicide plane. Several APDs were damaged. One APD was sunk by three suicide boats that managed to get through the picket patrol.

We could not see much of anything for we were covered with layers of smoke from our smoke making machines. And let me say now that I don't like either the theory or practice of this protective smoke business. You are just a sitting duck. You can't see to fire your own guns but you know the plane can see your outline. Once I heard a salvo of bombs drop near us and explode with a grim dry sound but we were covered with smoke and I could not see a damn thing.

Last night we experienced the same thing as the night before except that the Japs seemed to concentrate on the beach, and apparently with better results, for the fires around the airfields were pretty bright and burned for a long time.

One thing last night gave me the scare of my life. In the midst of all our smoke a plane dropped some bombs that exploded immediately, this followed by a peculiar odor that smelled like manure, and much like one of the gases we studied at Bradford. Also there was something similar to the smell of mustard gas, or so we thought.

I tell you I was plenty scared. Thought our time had come. Expected to keel over any minute but after a bit with no ill effects I knew I had been wrong. Everyone else thought much the same thing. They were all looking at me and I had to assume an air of indifference or we might have had a panic among the crew. I am glad to be away from Okinawa for a while anyway.

MAY 16

No entries because nothing has happened. We proceeded back to Ulithi and once there turned the crew out to pasture for 10 days.

This afternoon we get underway for Leyte, five LST's with an APD and a PC as escort. We are the first ship in column so it makes it nice for our helmsman and a little easier for me.

Ulithi was cooler this time and far more pleasant without the Army aboard crawling allover us, but I was once more glad to leave.

Hope the sea will remain calm. It is like a lake. Our biggest worry this time of year is the typhoon.

JUNE 7, EN ROUTE FROM LEYTE GULF

The Philippines were interesting. My trip to Manila remains the highlight of a three week stay, the rest of the time being spent in sleep or drinking beer and waiting for the letters from home.

Commander Anderson is a dolt and dunderhead in my opinion and I do not like being under the Coast Guard, but I guess we will get there all right.

There are 15 ships in this convoy carrying the stuff to build the stuff to fly the stuff to bomb the Japs. Won't be long before they start to stew in their own juice.

JUNE 18 OKINAWA AGAIN

On the 16th we delivered our second load at Hagushi. As pleasant and cooperative a group as we could hope to meet with. But the confusion prior to beaching was about as bad as any I have met within the war.

At 1000 we were told to anchor off Orange Beach, which we did. At about 1700 we received a message from the beach master saying, "What are you doing there we have no orders for you." So we pulled out to a safer anchorage being so close to an LST on the beach that the skipper must have been having palpitations of the heart.

At 1900 we received orders to beach at 2230. At 2230 we had an air attack and the harbor was so filled with smoke from the smoke generators that you could not see your hand *before your face.*

A salvo of bombs dropped so close to the ship that all of the Army officers got out of their sack. So you know it must have been close. Finally the smoke cleared out even though the lights on the beach were lit and we could not be sure where our slot was meant to be. It was described as the slot north of the highway on Orange I. But there were 5 runways running in all directions from the area around Orange I.

Sent in two small boats but they could not find the slot. They did meet up with an officer who said we could beach against some pontoons at 0200. So we dropped both anchors, fore and aft, just off the pontoons. At 0200 we were told to get underway. At 0211 we were told not to come in, that a load with higher priority was to use the pontoons.

I gave up. We dropped both anchors and stayed where we were. Next morning at 1100 we were told to beach immediately, which we did threading our path though a fleet of LCTs to tie up at the narrow pontoons.

Unloading went smoothly and at 2300 that night we retracted in the shadows of the night. Pretty hair raising but all went smoothly and we have now delivered our number 2 load.

Okinawa this trip was relatively calm with only about three real air raids in one week, and the fog generators not nearly as unpleasant as a result. The weather was so pleasant and cool I almost hated to leave this battle zone. But as Dugout Doug said, "I shall return."

JULY I, SAIPAN, ANOTHER ISLAND

The first few days a pleasant breeze blowing, making the air chilly at night. Lately it has' been hot and sultry Saipan is a center of frenzied activity. Allover the lsland supplies of every kind are piled. Crossing the highway here is like navigating Fifth Avenue at five in the afternoon. An endless flow of jeeps and trucks are streaming by 24 hours a day. I see many negro labor troops. The American war effort continues and I wonder for how long. I am feeling tired and lethargic, stale is the word, but there seems no end in view. How long can the young men stand this, this being separated from home and all one loves. Our leaders in the news say we will do this and that. We. Who will do it but we young men?

But Saipan goes on. The island is five to eight miles in

length, with a hill at the north end. There are still Japs on the island, though most of them have been rooted out or have surrendered.

Mail service is very good, but the orders to leave were a tonic to me. Sitting is pleasant for a while, but it gets hard after a week, just waiting, doing nothing, accomplishing nothing.

Another day is about over. How many will there be like this one?

JULY 20, SAIPAN

Nearly four weeks here, our longest stay at any port. They do not know what to do with us. The crew seems stale and tired.

We loaded some Australian and New Zealand meat at Leyte and that has not been too good. A long while since we had a good steak.

The officers club here is not much, and aside from that I found nothing to do but stay aboard ship. We would go crazy without the movies that are exchanged among our ships--the larger ships having the best supply of movies.

The afternoon of the 19th, yesterday, I received an order to report to Captain Wooden, II At my leisure. II I reported and was given a set of orders. Could hardly believe it. Pearl Harbor. Little did I think I would ever be so excited about anything. I could hardly talk. I told the crew that night before the movie and they nearly tore the deck off the ship.

You would have thought the war was over, and of course this means for us the war is over for several months, going back and forth with another load of men and equipment, probably for the invasion of Japan.

Thought we were all set this afternoon, then as we were about to get under way orders arrived delaying our sailing. It seemed the bottom had fallen out of everything. I felt sick at the stomach. An air of gloom pervaded our ship.

Sent Holland in to check and found we leave at 0800 tomorrow morning.

Won't believe we are at Pearl until we actually sail into the harbor. Seems too good to be true. I am going to bed waiting and praying.

JULY 21, AT SEA

Exhilarating to be at sea again, heading east into the trades and feeling the spray as it flies over the bow. After sitting at anchor for four weeks there is nothing like being under way, particularly when we are heading east. We are all rusty after being idle for so long. I felt nervous bringing the ship out of harbor, fearful that we would have some accident or collision that would delay or cancel our voyage. The helmsman was bad and even after we were clear of the harbor we nearly had a collision that would delay or cancel our orders, nearly hit an LSM. Finally when our convoy was formed up and really moving I felt a great sense of relief.

Gave a material inspection of the ship this morning that was the best we ever had. It was hard physically climbing all the ladders and going into all the crannies aboard a ship this size, but I feel it will help morale and our efficiency of operation.

This sea voyage should be a pleasant change. Am looking forward to it, as is everyone crew and officers. We have taken on a kind of collective personality.

AUGUST 14, PEARL HARBOUR

At last it has come. My God I thank Thee with all my heart.

At about 1400 Hawaiian time the radio gave word that the war was over. Japan has not signed the document of surrender but they have notified us through diplomatic channels that they capitulate completely.

The spirit and peace that comes over me is soft and soothing. At last it is over. These days of monotonous toiling and plodding with victory and peace a far off thing. Now they are here in our very grasp. There will be months of waiting to be discharged, but the great day is here. This is it. The news was greeted with the blowing of whistles from many ships, the sounding of general quarters and some bell ringing. But most of the steam was let off with the firing of rockets. Today everybody feels wonderful and let's it go at that.

AUGUST 27, MONDAY

At sea en route to Guam, we thought. Yesterday morning at 0515 awakened by the quartermaster who handed me a visual message just received from a destroyer in our convoy. Message read--"Proceed to Midway and await escort. Expect diversionary orders." This was about the most exciting thing that had ever happened to Lady Luck, LST 864. We had been en route to the Marshalls and then to Guam our fore deck loaded with creosoted telephone poles and a Marine Communications team on board. We imagined a long lazy voyage that would only be a retracing of our steps of six months before.

The only reason that our ship would be heading for Midway was that we were Tokyo bound. This was only a guess, where else could Midway lead? So for two days we have been surging along at flank-speed, alone on a wide, wide sea. The wind is from our starboard quarter, and causes us to roll pleasantly instead of beating the bow head against the waves.

Every night we have been showing a movie out in the open on the main deck. No blackout condition. Actually, we have only been authorized to use running lights and the supposition is that the ship will be otherwise blacked out, but my attitude is what the hell.

As long as we can't go home this is the next best excitement. (As I read this 45 years later I wonder what might have happened had a rogue Jap sub seen us, as perhaps was the case with the Indianapolis).

AUGUST 30

At 0415 I was notified that we had spotted the lights of Midway Island. Midway always had a thrilling sound to me as the result of the famous battle fought in 1942 in that vicinity. As I watched the speck grow into an island I looked forward to going ashore with anticipation.

A pilot and three tugs met us. Imagine all that preparation for the 864. It was the first time in months that we had been given a tug or pilot.

Later we learned that we were the first LST ever to come into Midway. We were treated with deference and I found here that being a commanding officer really meant something. I was given my own jeep and proceeded to make a tour of the island. It was a pretty little place. The buildings as part of a submarine base had an air of permanence in contrast to the drab quonset huts we had been seeing at advanced bases.

I got a glimpse of the gooney bird, silly bird that it is, related to the albatross. Regulations are strict and if you harm a Gooney bird all hell will break loose and you will likely get shot.

We did extremely well with supplies, obtaining fresh frozen vegetables, quantities of fresh oranges and other luxuries that we forgot existed.

A submarine skipper came aboard and I showed him around. He was amazed at the roominess of our landing ships and my quarters with my own bedroom, study and private bath.

Later he took me to the four striper in command of the submarine Tender Aegis, a huge ship moored across from us. The Captain gave us carte blanche to draw all the beer that we wanted from his ship. They had 1000 cases on board and will leave for the states in two days.

We learn that we are going great circle to Tokyo Bay, without going by way of Guam which would take a couple of weeks longer. We go in company with a PC, a little ship of only 180 feet. The two ships together and alone on the great Pacific.

TUESDAY, SEPTEMBER 4

On and on to Japan. Sea glassy and the wild following wind has shifted to our starboard quarter.

Yesterday afternoon we passed a mine 75 yards to port. The PC nearly hit but evidently did not see it. They went back to the mine and fired their 3 inch but missed, then returned to us. Cannot understand why they did not really attempt to explode the mine. Merely reporting it is not going to do a great deal of good.

SATURDAY, SEPTEMBER 8

About 470 miles to Yokosuka. Near here the Carrier Hornet launched the B-25s that took part in the Doolittle raid.

Also, through these waters the beaten Jap fleet retreated from Midway. Interesting to think what the sea has seen.

These must have been difficult waters for the old sailing ships, the wind is so variable. In the last 24 hours the wind has moved in a complete circle. The current is *against us and quite strong, slowing us down by a knot or more. Sky overcast much of the time, a northern sky. Sunsets are sharp and clear, like a Japanese picture. Colors are vivid and blend beautifully with grotesque cloud formations. A few land birds are finally making their appearance.*

We have seen no ships since leaving Midway and the sea is lonely. The last few days of a voyage are usually a strain, and this is no exception. Should have learned to relax by now.

THURSDAY, SEPTEMBER 27

At 0800 this morning we said goodbye to Yokosuka and Japan. Bound for Leyte we hope in an indefinite way that we are going to the states but so far it is just a hope.

We had a complicated time getting under way. Two of our men were stranded on an LSM. We did not know where. We sent the boat after them but at 0800 it had not returned.

Proceeding through the channel we had a steering casualty. Still no boat. At the end of the channel two small boats were attached together by an air line blocking our path. A diver was below. We nearly went aground dodging them.

Our small boat somehow found us and returned with the men. That was one good break, for the men and for me.

That afternoon the barometer started to drop. Finally it dropped 34 in 12 hours. Typhoon warnings were out on the radio.

To make matters worse our sea chests had apparently become blocked by marine growth and were not taking in enough salt water to cool our two diesel engines. Feared to slow to standard speed, about 6 knots. At 2300 the barometer bounced up. It is raining buckets. I have fingers crossed.

It did no good. We went through four hours of a typhoon that spun us around like a cork. But we survived. The workers back in Jeffersonville, Indiana can be proud, as we are grateful for their skill in welding the plates of 864.

OCTOBER 4

After the typhoon a week ago we enjoyed fine weather. We knew it was a typhoon, traveling alone as were, because any disturbance that causes the barometer to drop below 29 50 is accounted one. During our storm--typhoon, the barometer dropped to 29 29.

We had a formula for computing a safe course to follow when a typhoon hits. It had to do with finding the direction of the wind and then adding 180 degrees to find a safe course. If we had taken that course we would have ended up on a rocky island. We just banged forward straight ahead.

The men have done a good and energetic job repairing damage on the foredeck. Hope the paint will last. It is Japanese paint that we took from a warehouse at Yokusaka, by what we call cumshaw requisition, with the Japanese bowing and saluting all around us.

NOVEMBER 5, MONDAY

Since my last entry of October 4 we have made another run to Japan, this time to Nagasaki, where we are now.

Outside the Port Director's Office there must have been 3000 sailors, seabees and marines milling about in complete confusion. A seaman and warrant boatswain were in charge of the transportation program. Neither seemed to have had experience in that kind of work. Am writing this down because in after years it may seem only a kind of nightmare.

Sea bags, duffle bags, suitcases, and valpacs were strewn about like a wasteland after a volcanic eruption. No one complained because we were happy to be going home. I had departed my lovely ship LST 864 that morning. With a wife and two baby children, plus 36 months duty overseas I had mo~ than enough points for my release from active duty.

Now, after an hour of waiting, we were not a bit restless, happy at our good fortune at being about to board a ship for San Francisco.

The boatswain climbed aboard an LCT like once carried the foredeck of the 864, this LCT being tied up near the Port Director's Office.

Now the boatswain picked up an electric bullhorn, which chose that moment to go on the blink. The boatswain had looked haggard and tired before. Now he was forced to shout the list of hundreds of names from a mimeographed set of orders.

Our surging group was an immense crowd and it was difficult to hear your name. The point was that when you heard your name you threw your gear on the LCT and then *jumped aboard yourself.*

After a long wait I heard something that sounded like my name, so I jumped onto the steel deck on the LCT. After another hour of loading the LCT proceeded to a sleek gray ship of some 600 feet, APA 97, the Dolphin. May I never forget her name.

After some effort I lugged my four pieces of gear up the gangway, no longer a skipper having men to carry his baggage for him. I presented a copy of my orders to the officer of the deck, who could care less about another Navy Lieutenant in a rumpled khaki uniform. Although there were numerous men hanging around no effort was made to help any of us because we were going back to the States.

Our living compartment was a huge space of bunks on top of each other, four bunks to a tier that could not be triced and had to stay in place.

Our sheets were in a roll on my bunk and as I started to make them into a bed I discovered they were damp as hell, evidently having just come from the ship's laundry. Little did it matter. I was on my way to San Francisco.

We ate in shifts and if we had been assigned to a particular shift there would have been long waits for chow. The fact is that for 16 days we had nothing to do but wait, so what did it matter.

Salt water showers are all that is available, and I suppose we are lucky to get them. Everything seems too good to be true, so much so that I am keeping my fingers crossed that we will not hit a mine. Having progressed this far on my journey to the States alive and without injury it seems a bit of an accomplishment.

NOVEMBER 10

My fifth day aboard the Dolphin, our fourth day underway. As the great circle course we follow takes us north to Latitude 50 degrees, as compared to 38 degrees at. Jeffersonville it is becoming colder . . . and those of us who have just left the tropics feel it.

We eat in three sittings, but unassigned, first come first served. Our meals are hurried but the grub is good under the circumstances. The main hardship is not the food or the cold or the lack of fresh water but the fact that I can never get a chance to read. All space is so crowded that we have no privacy. So what the hell. I have been spoiled by my wonderful quarters about LST 864.

NOVEMBER, 22

The sight of Golden Gate Bridge is all I need enter today.

DECEMBER 5

In Charleston, South Carolina waiting to get my physical and my papers of demobilization, orders to inactive duty I should say.

My wife and son and daughter and all grandparents are well. All OK except for the presumed death of my brother-in-law, 19 year old Sandy James, whose plane was shot down over Burma. For me the war is over.

* * * * * * * * * *

U.S. NAVY AMPHIBIOUS SHIPS DESTROYED DURING WORLD WAR II

CATEGORY: LANDING SHIP, TANK (LST)

USS LST-6	Sunk by a mine in the Seine River while en route from Rouen, France, to Portland, England, 18 November 1944.
USS LST-43	Sunk by explosion at Pearl Harbor, Hawaii, 21 May 1944.
USS LST-69	Sunk by explosion at Pearl Harbor, Hawaii, 21 May 1944.
USS LST-158	Sunk by aircraft off Licata, Sicily, 11 July 1943.
USS LST-167	Stricken after being damaged beyond repair by Japanese aircraft off Vella Lavella, Solomon Islands, 25 September 1943.
USS LST-179	Sunk by explosion at Pearl Harbor, Hawaii, 21 May 1944.
USS LST-203	Destroyed by grounding near Nanumea, Ellice Islands, 2 October 1943.
USS LST-228	Destroyed by grounding near Bahia Angra Island, Azores, 21 January 1944.
USS LST-282	Sunk by a glider bomb off St. Tropez, France, 15 August 1944.
USS LST-313	Sunk by German aircraft off Gela, Sicily, 10 July 1943.
USS LST-314	Sunk by German motor torpedo boats off Normandy, France, 9 June 1944.
USS LST-318	Sunk by aircraft off Caronia, Sicily, 10 August 1943.
USS LST-333	Sunk by German submarine U-593 off Dellys, Algeria, 22 June 1943.
USS LST-342	Sunk by Japanese submarine RO-106 west of Guadalcanal, Solomon Islands, 18 July 1943.
USS LST-348	Sunk by German submarine U-410 off Anzio, Italy, 20 February 1944.
USS LST-349	Sunk after running aground off Ponza, Italy, 26 February 1944.
USS LST-353	Sunk by internal explosion at Pearl Harbor, Hawaii, 21 May 1944.

USS LST-359	Sunk by German submarine U-870 northeast of the Azores, 20 December 1944.
USS LST-376	Sunk by German motor torpedo boats off Normandy, France, 9 June 1944.
USS LST-396	Sunk by accidental fire and explosion off Vella Lavella, Solomon Islands, 18 August 1943.
USS LST-447	Sunk by Kamikaze attack off Okinawa, Ryukyu Islands, 7 April 1945.
USS LST-448	Sunk by Japanese aircraft off Bougainville, Solomon Islands, 5 October 1943.
USS LST-460	Sunk by Kamikaze attack off Mindoro, Philippine Islands, 21 December 1944.
USS LST-472	Sunk by Kamikaze attack off Mindoro, Philippine Islands, 15 December 1944.
USS LST-480	Sunk by explosion at Pearl Harbor, Hawaii, 21 May 1944.
USS LST-493	Destroyed after grounding while attempting to enter Plymouth Harbor, England, 12 April 1945.
USS LST-496	Sunk by a mine off Normandy, France, 11 June 1944.
USS LST-499	Sunk by a mine off Normandy, France, 8 June 1944.
USS LST-507	Sunk by German motor torpedo boats in Lyme Bay, England, 28 April 1944.
USS LST-523	Sunk by a mine off Normandy, France, 19 June 1944.
USS LST-531	Sunk by German motor torpedo boats in Lyme Bay, England, 28 April 1944.
USS LST-563	Destroyed off Clipperton Island, southwest Pacific, 22 December 1944, and abandoned, 9 February 1945.
USS LST-577	Sunk by Japanese submarine RO-50 east of Mindanao, Philippine Islands, 11 February 1945.
USS LST-675	Destroyed off Okinawa, Ryukyu Islands, 4 April 1945, and abandoned, 17 September 1945..
USS LST-738	Sunk by Kamikaze aircraft off Mindoro, Philippine Islands, 15 December 1944.
USS LST-749	Sunk by Kamikaze aircraft off Mindoro, Philippine Islands, 21 December 1944.
USS LST-750	Sunk by Japanese aircraft off Los Negros, Leyte, Philippine Islands, 28 December 1944.

USS LST-808	Destroyed after being damaged by Japanese aircraft off Ie Shima, Ryukyu Islands, 18 May 1945, and destroyed, 11 November 1945.
USS LST-906	Destroyed off Leghorn, Italy, 18 October 1944, and scrapped, 22 June 1945.
USS LST-921	Torpedoed by German submarine U-764 off the channel entrance to Bristol, England, 14 August 1944, and struck from the Navy list, 14 October 1944.

****

SOURCE: *Department of the Navy, Naval Historical Center, 805 Kidder Breese SE, Washington Navy Yard, Washington, DC 20374-5060*

CHAPTER 8

REUNIONS OF LST-864 SHIPMATES

In late 1993, G/M 3C Frank Burns first began to plan for a reunion of the former crewmen of the USS LST-864. He had stayed in contact with a few former shipmates from his two tours of duty on the ship, but he felt the need for even more personal contact than that. With the help of his computer guru neighbor, after almost 2 1/2 years of searching he was able to contact around 25 members of the crew. After over 50 years without contact, locating former shipmates is much more difficult than it might initially seem.

The First USS LST-864 Reunion was scheduled for October 17-19, 1996, at the Biloxi Beach Motor Inn in Biloxi, Mississippi. Most of the men who had been contacted were extremely appreciative to know that a reunion of their former shipmates had been scheduled. Hosted by Frank and Ellie Burns, 17 of the 25 located shipmates and their wives turned out for the event.

Those who participated found themselves more touched by the reunion than they would have imagined. While it is clearly true that "time and tide stop for no man," the reunion proved that memories of days like those the men had spent together in their youth can last a lifetime. Many hugs and tears were exchanged on that good evening, and the reunion turned out to be a great success. One of the highlights of the evening was that Frank Burns was honored for the effort he had put into organizing the affair.

Reunions have taken place each year since 1996, hosted by various members of the crew in different cities or states. The reunion of 2001, for example, will be a voyage in the Bahamas out of Cape Canaveral on the cruise ship "The Sovereign of the Seas." Each year, new crewmen are found and invited to the annual gathering. When one of the crew passes away, he is remembered by each of his buddies.

The impact of any war--especially one as far-reaching as World War II--can last for many generations. Today, wives sometimes attend the reunion in memory of husbands who have passed away and sons and daughters attend in memory of their fathers. It is an activity that truly fills an emotional need, one shared not only by the crewmen themselves but also by members of their families. It has become a way of saying that the many sacrifices of the young men who served on the U.S.S. LST-864 have not been forgotten.

USS LST 864 CREW REUNIONS AS OF 2002

REUNION	DATE	LOCATION
First	October 17-19, 1996	Biloxi Beach Motor Inn Biloxi, Mississippi HOSTS: Frank & Ellie Burns
Second	October 17-19, 1997	Biloxi Beach Motor Inn Biloxi, Mississippi HOSTS: Frank & Ellie Burns
Third	October 5-7, 1998	Biloxi Beach Motor Inn Biloxi, Mississippi HOSTS: Gene & Bill Hanley
Fourth	November 5-7, 1999	Kissimmee, Florida HOSTS: Frank & Ellie Burns
Fifth	October 12-15, 2000	Ramada Inn--Riverside Jeffersonville, Indiana HOSTS: Ray & Lollie Keeler and Bill & Rose Mueller
Sixth	October 28-November 1, 2001	Cruise on the "Sovereign of the Seas," Cape Canaveral, Florida HOSTS: Jim & Beverly Lipinski
Seventh	October 9-12, 2002	Ramada Hotel Mobile, Alabama HOSTS: Frank & Ellie Burns and Jim & Beverly Lipinski

REUNIONS OF LST-864 SHIPMATES

The following photograph was taken as 14 members of a crew of 120 stood at the head of the launch ways at Jeffboat, Inc., in Jeffersonville, Indiana, the site from which they boarded "The Lady Luck" 23 years earlier to depart for service in the Pacific campaign against Japan and Germany during World War II. Some of the men boarded at Jeffersonville; others boarded as the ship was taken down river to New Orleans. Full scale reunions began in 1996. They have been going on ever since.

INFORMAL LST-864 REUNION
JEFFERSONVILLE, INDIANA
December 8, 1967

From left are Bill Mueller and John E. Hammond, both of St. Louis, MO; Gene Bittiker, Salisbury, MO.; Gayle Jacobson, Paul's Valley, OK; Don Emmel, Beaver Falls, PA; Julius Swope, Gettysburg, PA.; Joseph P. Dobesh, Minneapolis, MN; Jerry M. Dunman, Baytown, TX.; CPO Walter O. Rushing, Memphis, TN; Harold Bausman, Franklin, OH; Herbert O. Tinlin, Carrollton, OH; Glen Oval "Rosie" Rose, Defiance, OH; I. N. Pitts, Florence, AL, and Captain Richard B. Wathen of Jeffersonville, IN. Wathen was the first commander of the ship.

INFORMAL USS LST-864 REUNION AT JEFFERSONVILLE, INDIANA

This photograph of Crewman Issac Newton Pitts, Jr. (left), Chief Boatswain's Mate Walter O. Rushing (Center), and Captain Richard B. Wathen was taken on December 7, 1967, at a small and informal gathering of a few LST-864 shipmates, long before the first all-crew reunion was scheduled

LST-864 REUNITES FOR FIRST TIME

On October 17, 18 and 19, 1996, the crew of 17 shipmates and wives held their first reunion in Biloxi, MS. After searching for two and a half years, we found 25 old shipmates, then I made plans for our reunion. I have never been to Biloxi, but thought it would be a great place for all of us to get together because of location and the entertainment that would be available. I made all arrangements by phone, then kept my fingers crossed hoping that every-thing would turn out well. We stayed at the Biloxi Beach Resort Inn, and couldn't have made a better choice as they made our stay most enjoyable. We had a terrific hospitality room all set up for our group, and were able to furnish our own food and drinks. Kitty Barq who was in charge of sales did everything she could to make our reunion turn out to be a big success. In fact, we are going back in October '97 for our next reunion. If any of you LST organizers want some good information on holding a reunion in Biloxi, just give me a call. (941-933-1921). I will be glad to help you. Our first night, we had the hospitality room open, and we all got to meet after so many years. As you can probably guess, there were a lot of hugs and tears and a feeling that I cannot describe. I know for sure that I wouldn't have missed it for any-thing. Outside the door leading into the hospitality room I hung a sign that read: "Through these doors pass the men of the LST 864, who sailed the south Pacific in the year of 1944.

We were proud of out country, our flag and our ship, and we sailed her home on our very last trip. Under the Golden Gate Bridge we passed, thank God we were home, home at last." We had a table of honor set up in memory of our departed shipmates and after a prayer and a toast, we played taps and gave them a final salute. We had the honor. of having one of the widows with us; Jean Wick, who came from Sheboygan, WI. We were so happy that she came to join us for the reunion, that we made her an Honorary Ship Crew Member. On the second day, after a great continental breakfast, we board- ed buses to take us down to the docks for a pleasant boat ride around the harbor. After the boat ride, we walked into the Isle of Capri Casino for a terrific seafood buffet. That evening we all met back in the hospi- tality room for more party time, and through the VFW in Biloxi, I was able to find a one-man band so we could use the dance floor. He was really just great, and everyone really enjoyed his music and his singing.

The next day was a day to do whatever you felt like doing, and that is just what everyone did. That evening we all got dressed up and took a short walk from the motel to Landry's Seafood Restaurant for our ship reunion banquet. We had a private room for our dinner, and the menu even had our ships name at the top of it. Both Landry's Seafood Restaurant and Biloxi Beach Resort Inn had our ship's name on their Marquee. So, a lot of people in Biloxi knew the

864 was in town. After our banquet dinner we all had returned to the hospitality room to take some group pictures and video to r6member our reunion. A lot of good-byes were said then, as some of the folks were going to leave early in the morning. After making all of these arrangements by phone, it couldn't have turned out any better than it did. If you have a chance to go to a reunion for the first time, take my advice, and don't miss seeing your old buddies after so many years. Words cannot describe the feeling you will experience when you all get together. All of us from the old 864 are really looking forward to next reunion, and we are going to search as hard as we can for more shipmates to join us. I feel we have been very lucky to have found 25 shipmates in only two years of searching. We hope that some of our shipmates that didn't make our first reunion will be able to make the second one in October of 1997. It takes a lot of hard work trying to find your old buddies, but it can be done. It was really great looking at all the old pictures that the fellows brought with them. I forgot what good-looking sailors we were, and especially how slim and trim we were. LST sailing was pretty good duty, even if they were rough riding at times. The small crew made us feel close to one another, and we knew everyone by name. It was nice coming into a harbor and sailing past the big fighting ships as they were holding personal inspection on deck and we were wearing cut-off jeans and straw hats. We didn't have to ride a liberty boat for an hour to the beach for a beer party, as our captain just put the ship right on the beach. I bet a lot of you old LST sailors can even remember opening the bow' doors and lowering the ramp for skinny-dipping parties. Skinny dipping with a cold beer- those were the days, ha, ha! I guess of all the ships duty you could have, being on an LST wasn't too bad. We were just as proud of our ship as the sailors on the big fighting ships. When they finished blasting the islands, it was the LSTers who took the men and supplies right onto the beach. Don't miss your next ship reunion, as we may not have many left-we aren't getting any younger.

Frank J. Burns G/M 3C
USS LST 864
"Lady Luck"

SOURCE: LST Scuttlebutt, January/February 1977, Page 38

FIRST USS LST-864 REUNION
BILOXI, MISSISSIPPI -- OCTOBER 17-19, 1996

LADY LUCK
U.S.S. L.S.T. 864 U.S. NAVY
52 YR REUNION
1944 — 1996

Through these doors pass the men of the L.S.T. 864
Who sailed the South Pacific in the year of 1944
We were proud of our Country, our Flag, and our Ship
And we sailed it home on our very last trip
Under the Golden Gate Bridge we passed
Thank God we were Home, Home, Home at Last

BACK ROW (STANDING) - Gene Hanley, Leanard Swazey, Nathaniel McCloud, Bill Reed, Jim Lipinski, Roman Berzinski, Frank Bums and Joe Dobesh. SEATED - Joe Terry, Harold Bausman, Bill Mueller, Captain Richard "Dick" Wathen, Merle Bauer, Julius Swope, Walter Bertouille, and Bill Hanley. FRONT ROW (SEATED ON FLOOR) - Honorary Crew Member Jean Wick (holding sign).

Frank Kidd, Bill Reed, Ray Keeler, Joe Dobesh, Frank Burns, Jack Caldie and Claude Jewell (Kneeling)

REUNIONS OF LST-864 SHIPMATES

Pictured from Left to Right at the 1996 LST-864 Reunion: (Standing, Left to Right) Sue Reed, Priscilla McCloud, Dorothy Bauer, Aleene Terry, Jean Wick, Loretta Keeler, Thelma Berzinski; (Seated) Betty Dobesh, Rose Mueller, Margaret Swazey, Bev Lipinski, Eleanor Burns, and Charlotte Swope.

Frank Burns (Left) and Captain Richard B. Wathen at the 1996 LST-864 Reunion

Master of Ceremonies Frank Burns (Right) honoring Captain Richard B. Wathen. LST-864 Reunion of 1996.

Merle Bauer and Captain Richard Wathen

Frank Burns, recipient of a plaque of recognition for having organized the first LST-864 Reunion in 1996

SECOND USS LST-864 REUNION
BILOXI, MISSISSIPPI -- OCTOBER 17-19, 1997

TOP ROW - Jim Lipinski, Joe Terry, Frank Burns, Ray Keeler, and Roman "Breezy" Berzinski. MIDDLE ROW - Bill Mueller, Joe Dobesh, William Reed, Merle Bauer, and Walter Bertoulle. FRONT ROW - Gene Hanley and Bill Hanley.

USS LST-864 --LADY LUCK

On October 5 through 7, the 864 held its third reunion in Biloxi, MS. This was the third year we stayed at the same hotel, and it was only about a week after hurricane George hit that area. After the storm, we weren't sure that we would be able to hold our reunion there, because of possible damage. We held our breath and then a few days before our reunion date, we found out that we could be put up at the hotel. This year out reunion was hosted by Gene and Bill Hanley, who by the way, were twin brothers (officers) who served aboard ship with us. We were honored to have with us our Captain Richard Wathen, who was at our first get together, but missed the second reunion as he was feeling under the weather. It was great to see him back again this time, and our hats are off to him for being there with us all. I did some searching this last year for old shipmates, and with the help of a great neighbor, Roy Shramm, we found 18 old shipmates from the 864.

Six of them made it to this reunion and really had a great time. Three had to cancel, and we missed them very much. Roy Shramm, my neighbor, has a computer to work with, and that's how we found the new shipmates. One of, the new men we found was another officer by the name of Welbur Gibson, who was able to join us with his wife Marge. Also, we were honored to have with us for the first time, Fred and Jean Andrews, Dave and Betty Ellis, Claude Jewell, Jack Denton arid Jack Caldie. I am sure they all had a wonderful time, because they thanked me more then once for finding them. They can't, be any more happier then I that we found them, and could be with us for this reunion. The Hanley brothers, that hosted the party, did a great job by starting off our hospitality night with pizza, drinks and snacks. Boy, what a great time we had that night, especially having our newly found shipmates with us for the first time. I heard so many stories of things that happened that I didn't remember, that I wonder if I was on the same ship. Ha ha. Well, after a night of lots of fun, we turned in to get ready for the next day. We all had a continental breakfast furnished by the hotel Then we all climbed aboard a bus for a trip to New Orleans. We had lunch at one of the oldest restaurants in New Orleans, Tujagues. After a nice lunch, we went aboard a paddle-wheel boat for a ride on the river. Then it was back to the hotel, and off to the casinos. The next day we had a meeting to decide on what to do for next year. We all seemed to want a change, so I volunteered to host next years reunion in Kissimmee, FL. From our first reunion, a feeling of respect, love, togetherness, many more things.

have grown more and more each year. We can't wait to see each other when reunion time rolls around, and now we all have something to look forward to each year. Missing from our reunion this year, and missed by all of us were the following shipmates. Leonard and Marie Swazey, Nathaniel and Priscilla McCloud, and Bill and Sue Reed. We all hope to see them next year at our fourth reunion in Kissimee, FL. I have talked to a lot of ex-service men that have never had a chance to go to a reunion and meet their old buddies. They all said that they would give anything to be able to have that opportunity, but no one ever got one started. If you are one of the old crew members from the 864, and haven't been to one of our reunions, you don't know what you are missing. At our age we don't have too many years left, so if you are able to join us at our next reunion don't miss an opportunity of a life time. We would love to have as many of our old shipmates as possible join us for the time of their lives.

Now, back to our reunion, to say that on our last night in Biloxi, we had our banquet dinner right at the hotel, and it was enjoyed by all. After our dinner, we took a lot of pictures of each other to remember our big party. Now everyone is looking forward to coming to Florida in November, 1999. On our last morning, a lot of good-byes were said again during a continental breakfast furnished by the hotel. Thanks again to the Hanley brothers for hosting our third reunion, and making it a big success.

Oh, you probably noticed that our banner in the picture said second reunion. When I changed the dates, I forgot to change it to the third. Getting old I guess. Someone told me that if I was questioned about it, just say it was the second reunion from the first one. That sounded good so I'll buy it. Ha ha.

I'll do some more searching for old buddies this coming year, and with some luck we may have a bigger reunion the next time around. So until next year, I want to say to all the LSTer's that read this, to keep on having your reunions as long as you can, and for each new shipmate that you find you will be bringing happiness to another old buddy. He will say "My God they have found me at last."

G/M/3c Frank Burns

SOURCE: LST-864 Scuttlebutt, January/February 1999, Page 50

THIRD USS LST-864 REUNION
BILOXI, MISSISSIPPI - OCTOBER 5-7, 1998

TOP ROW (STANDING) - Fred Andrews, Frank Burns, Roman "Breezy" Berzinski, Dave Ellis, Jim Lipinski, and Jack Caldie. CENTER ROW (SITTING) - Welbur Gibson, Joe Debesh, Joe Terry, Honorary Crew Member Jean Wick, Bill Mueller, Julius Swope, and Bill Hanley. FRONT ROW (FLOOR) - Unnamed, Gene Hanley, Claude Jewell, Merle Bauer and Ray Keeler. NOTE: The banner in the photograph is mislabeled; this was the third reunion.

SPOUSES OF
USS LST 864 CREWMEN THIRD REUNION
BILOXI, MI - OCTOBER 5-7, 1998

Pictured from Left to Right: (Front Row, Sitting) - Rose Mueller, Aleene Terry, Eleanor Burns, Thelma Bresinski, Charlotte Swope, and Betty Ellis; (Back Row, Standing) - Dorothy Bauer, Lollie Keeler, Marge Gibson, Jean Andrews, Jean Wick, and Betty Dobesh.

FOURTH LST-864 REUNION
KISSIMMEE, FLORIDA
NOVEMBER 5-7, 1999

Welbur Gibson, Frank Burns, Joe Dobesh, William Provins, Jim Lipinski, Merle Bauer, Julius Swope, Joe Terry and Bill Mueller.

FIFTH LST-864 REUNION
JEFFERSONVILLE, INDIANA
OCTOBER 12-15, 2000

BACK ROW (STANDING) - Gene Hanley, Joe Dobesh, Julius Swope, Roman "Breezy" Berzinski, Nathanial McCloud, Fred Andrews, Joe Terry, Merle Bauer, and Ray Keller. CENTER ROW (SITTING) - Jim Lipinski, Welbur Gibson, Captain Richard Wathen, Dave Ellis, William Reed, and Bill Mueller. FRONT ROW (KNEELING) - Claude Jewell, Frank Burns, and Bill Hanley.

SIXTH LST-864 REUNION
CAPE CANAVERAL, FLORIDA
October 28 - November 1, 2001

TOP ROW - Jim Lipinski. SECOND ROW - Roman "Breezy" Berzinski and Claude Jewell. THIRD - Malcom Kaehler, Unnamed, and Frank Burns. FOURTH ROW - Bill Reed and Joe Dobesh. FIFTH ROW (BOTTOM) - Julius Swope and Bill Mueller.

SPOUSES OF CREWMEN AT THE SIXTH LST-864 REUNION CAPE CANAVERAL, FLORIDA
October 28 - November 1, 2001

FRONT ROW - Charlotte Swope and Rose Mueller. SECOND ROW - Sue Reed, Betty Dobesh, and Jean Wick. THIRD ROW- Freddie Kaehler, Beverly Lipinski, and Thelma Berzinski. FOURTH ROW - Guest, Jean Andrews, Eleanor Burns and Aleene Terry. TOP ROW - Guest.

MEMORIAL WREATH-LAYING AT SEA DURING THE 2001 REUNION

CREWMEN LAYING A WREATH AT SEA IN MEMORY OF CAPTAIN WATHEN AND ALL OTHER DEPARTED SHIPMATES.

Joe Dobesh, Jim Lipinski, Roman "Breezy" Berzinski and Bill Reed.

SEVENTH LST-864 REUNION
MOBILE, ALABAMA -- OCTOBER 9-12, 2002

TOP ROW - Michael Dreese, Joe Dobesh, Ron Miller, Roman Berzinski, Frank Kidd, Mike Keeler (Guest), Fred Andrews, Claude Jewell, Bill Mueller, Jim Lipinski, Tony Ganss (Guest), Julius Swope, and Welbur Gibson. MIDDLE ROW - Frank Burns, Bill Reed, Ray Keeler, Merle Bauer and Bill Provins. FRONT ROW - Malcolm Kaehler, Bill Hanley, Jean Wick (honorary crew member) and Gene Hanley. NOT PICTURED - David White and Odd White (Dave White's son).

SEVENTH LST-864 REUNION
MOBILE, ALABAMA
OCTOBER 9-12, 2002

TOP ROW - Rose Mueller, Charlotte Swope, Betty Dobesh, Lolly Keeler, Neva Dreese, Thelma Berzinski, Jean Wick, Ellie Burns, Dorothy Bauer, Freddie Kaehler, Gail Kidd, Jean Andrews, Betty Miller and Peg Hanley.
BOTTOM ROW - Bev Lipinski, Sue Reed, Merle Bauer, Susie Bauer; Geneva Provins, Marge Gibson and Mary Hanley.

VISIT TO THE LST MEMORIAL SHIP
THE USS LST-325 IN MOBILE, ALABAMA

The main attraction of the 2002 LST-864 Reunion was a visit to see the LST Memorial Ship, the USS LST-325. Hosted by members of the blue crew on duty that day at work on the restoration, LST-864 crewmen and their wives were treated to a complete tour of old ship. Everyone enjoyed the visit and being aboard brought back a lot of memories. The restoration project is moving along nicely, and one day the LST-325 will sail with pride once again. The finished project will serve a living memorial to the role the LSTs and their crews played in World War II.

On the deck of the LST Memorial Ship, LST-325

REUNIONS OF LST-864 SHIPMATES

Pictured aboard LST-325 - Jim Lipinski, Bill Mueller, Joe Dobesh, Claude Jewell, and Merle Bauer

Frank Burns presenting a donation on behalf of LST-864 crewmen to Cal Ellison, blue crew member, LST-325 Memorial Ship Restoration Fund

*Seaman's Bunks Aboard the LST-325 Memorial Ship.
Bunks on the USS LST-864 were similar.*

REUNIONS OF LST-864 SHIPMATES

*Welbur Gibson (Left) and Merle Bauer
in the galley of the LST-325 Memorial Ship*

CONNING TOWER AND DECK VIEW
OF THE LST MEMORIAL SHIP, THE USS LST-325

*Conning Tower
Of the USS LST-325*

*Welbur Gibson (Left),
Gene Hanley, and Bill Hanley
aboard the USS LST-325*

*Topside view of the LST-325 Memorial Ship.
Note that the ship is, in effect, a construction site*

Boarding the USS LST-325 memorial ship at dockside

Bill Reed in the galley of the LST-325

CHAPTER 9

THANKS FOR A JOB WELL DONE

Personal sacrifice has always been the price of war, and the men who served aboard the LST-864 were in no way exempt from this reality. Some of their sacrifices were apparent, but many of their struggles were subtle and more difficult to observe and quantify. Regardless of the many different shades and forms of hardship they endured, their sacrifices were many and they were all very real.

First and foremost, they were in constant danger of loosing their lives in armed conflict at sea. The battle record clearly shows that LST-864's crewmen were on repeated occasions in mortal danger of being fired upon or shelled from the land, bombed at sea, or sunk by Japanese submarines. All of them say without hesitation that they were afraid for their very lives on more than one occasion. Only by happenstance were crewmen not wounded or killed or their ship sunk to the bottom of the sea. When the look back to consider the record of sea miles logged by the ship and the times they were near danger, the men are thankful to God that they were able to accomplish their various missions and return home alive.

Secondly, the general stress of military service was a constant threat to the mental and emotional health of the men. They knew very well that some of them might not get through the war alive and well, and this very fact at times caused them to behave in ways they wouldn't have under normal circumstances. Many of them concluded their term of service addicted to nicotine, alcohol, lifestyle or attitudinal or behavioral changes, or related kinds of personal problems, all of which were not readily or immediately attributable to the pressures of war but, in fact, were. Some were changed for life by their experiences in the military.

Third, time away from loved ones and others who depended on them was the toughest kind of personal sacrifice to endure. It took the form of husbands being away from wives, fathers being away from their children, sons separated from their sometimes elderly and needful parents, workers being away from jobs, or entrepreneurs being away from businesses that needed them. At one time or another, all the men spent miserable days and nights immersed in loneliness or worry over concerns of this kind. Sacrifice of this kind is personal and, therefore, usually not readily observable, but it still was very real.

Fourth, the opportunity costs of involvement in military service have always been considerable, even though they cannot be precisely calculated. What price, for example, should be placed on an education not completed, on-the-job training opportunities lost, a great job not taken, a business opportunity not pursued, or an investment never made? Those who didn't serve in the military during the war years were spared this kind of personal sacrifice.

In summary, the young men who served on the LST-864 made all these as well as many other kinds of sacrifices on behalf of their country, as did all the other men who performed military service during World War II. When the conflict ended, the whole country knew that they were owed great respect and gratitude. Upon returning to their homes, they received the applause of a grateful nation--and they deserved it fully. Today, it is only right and proper to say to them once again: *"Thanks for a job well done!"*

Ensigns Peter and Hanley and Captain Wathen in Tokyo

Signed at TOKYO BAY, JAPAN at ____
on the SECOND day of SEPTEMBER, 1945.

重光葵
By Command and in behalf of the Emperor of Japan and the Japanese Government.

梅津美治郎
By Command and in behalf of the Japanese Imperial General Headquarters.

Accepted at TOKYO BAY, JAPAN at 0908 I
on the SECOND day of SEPTEMBER, 1945, for the United States, Republic of China, United Kingdom and the Union of Soviet Socialist Republics, and in the interests of the other United Nations at war with Japan.

Douglas MacArthur
Supreme Commander for the Allied Powers.

C.W. Nimitz
United States Representative

徐永昌
Republic of China Representative

Bruce Fraser
United Kingdom Representative

Kuzma Derevyanko
Union of Soviet Socialist Republics Representative

T.A. Blamey
Commonwealth of Australia Representative

L. Moore Cosgrave
Dominion of Canada Representative

Le Clerc
Provisional Government of the French Republic Representative

C.E.L. Helfrich
Kingdom of the Netherlands Representative

Leonard M. Isitt
Dominion of New Zealand Representative

The Japanese surrender was signed aboard the USS Missouri.

Japanese Surrender Party

American designee, signing the surrender agreement.

Japanese designee, signing the surrender agreement.

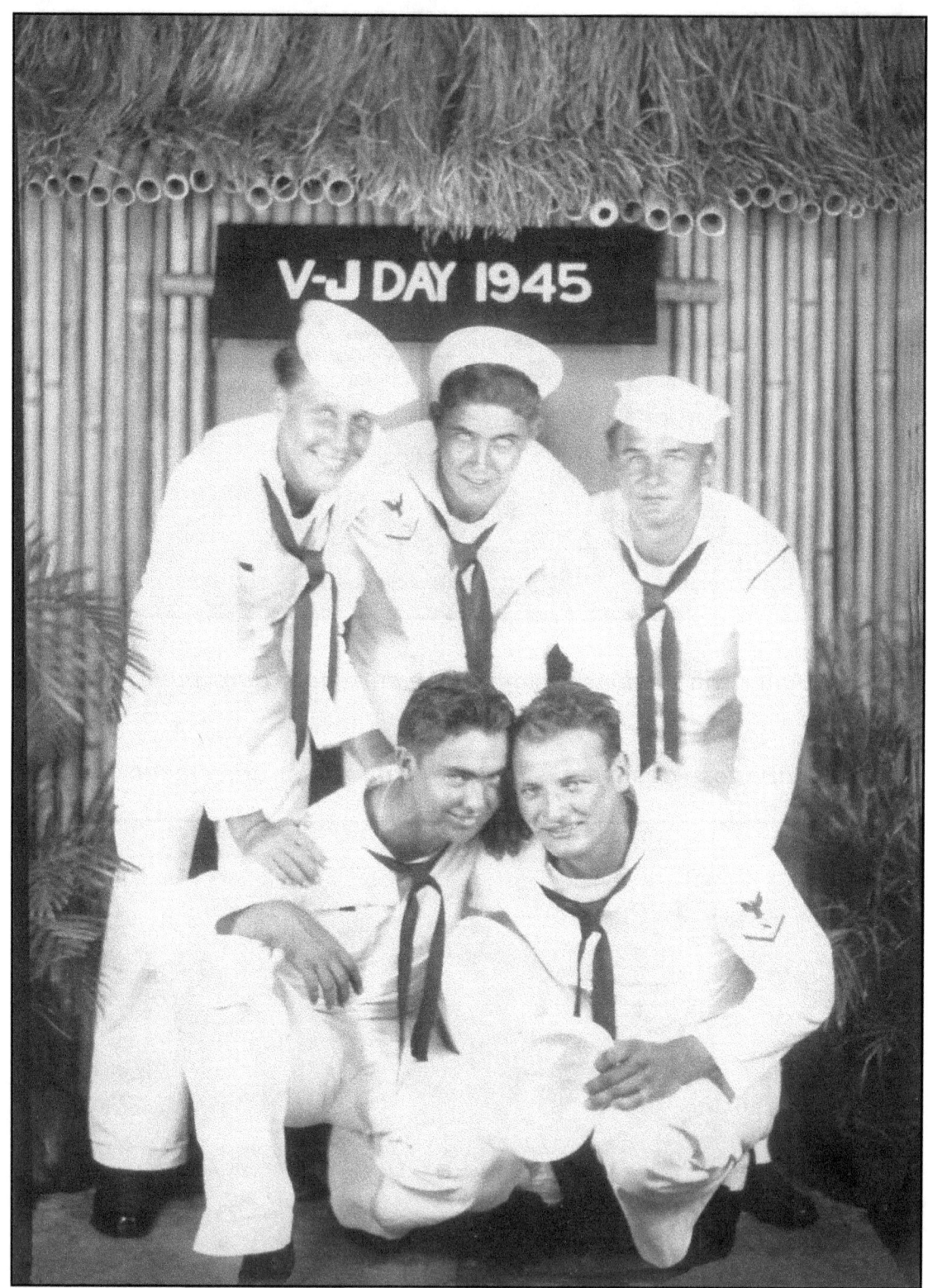

CREWMEN ON LIBERTY CELEBRATING VJ DAY
Top: Frank Burns, Leonard Swazey, and Unnamed;
Bottom -- H. E. Bullington and Roman Berzinski.

Sailors on leave celebrating VJ Day. Leonard Swazey (far right) and Roman Berzinski (second from right); others unnamed

John Maher (left) and Art Knutson, celebrating being discharged from the Navy in May of 1946

THE LADY LUCK

Wilbur Brandmair, Norman Porter, and Joe Dobesh, on VJ Day

Crewmen celebrating VJ Day in Honolulu

LST-864 SUPERLATIVES

Nathaniel McCloud, one of the youngest men aboard ship

Frank Bunker, one of the youngest men aboard ship

John Paul "Pops" Gainor, oldest man aboard ship

Joe Dobesh, longest serving crewman

"WHAT THE FIGHT WAS ALL ABOUT!"

John P. "Pops" Gainor of Coatsville, Pennsylvania, on leave in 1944, with wife Sarah and son Paul. Every serviceman had a family back at home, anxiously awaiting his return.

"SWEET LIBERTY"

Robert Jackson Martin, on leave. Shown with wife, Mary, and father, George Jackson Martin

Mary (Edwards) Martin of Hoffman, Oklahoma, in 1944

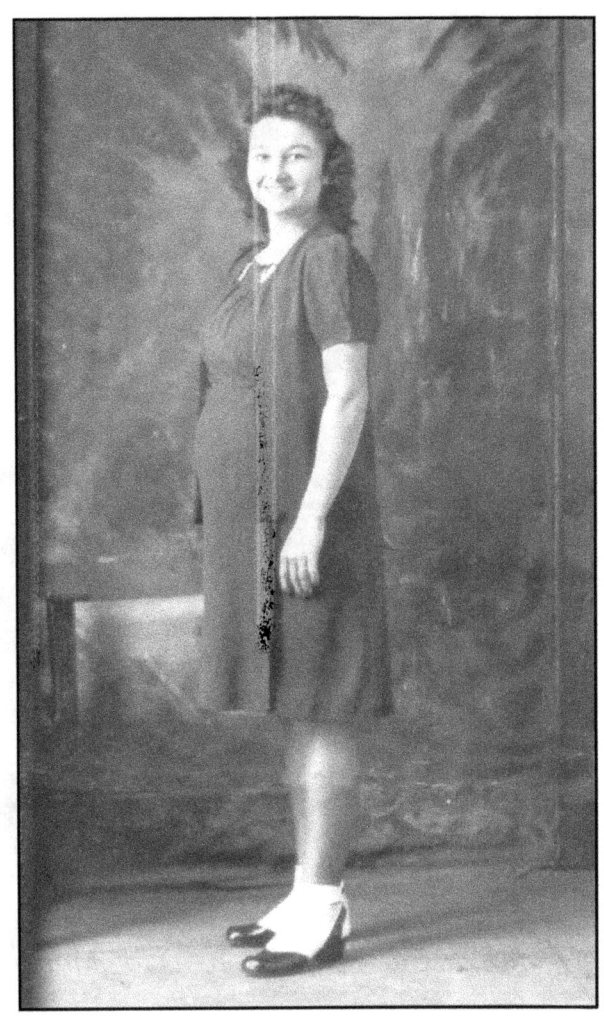

Robert Jackson "Bob" Martin, age 21, of Hoffman, Oklahoma

THANKS FOR A JOB WELL DONE

EVERY SERVICEMAN'S DREAM

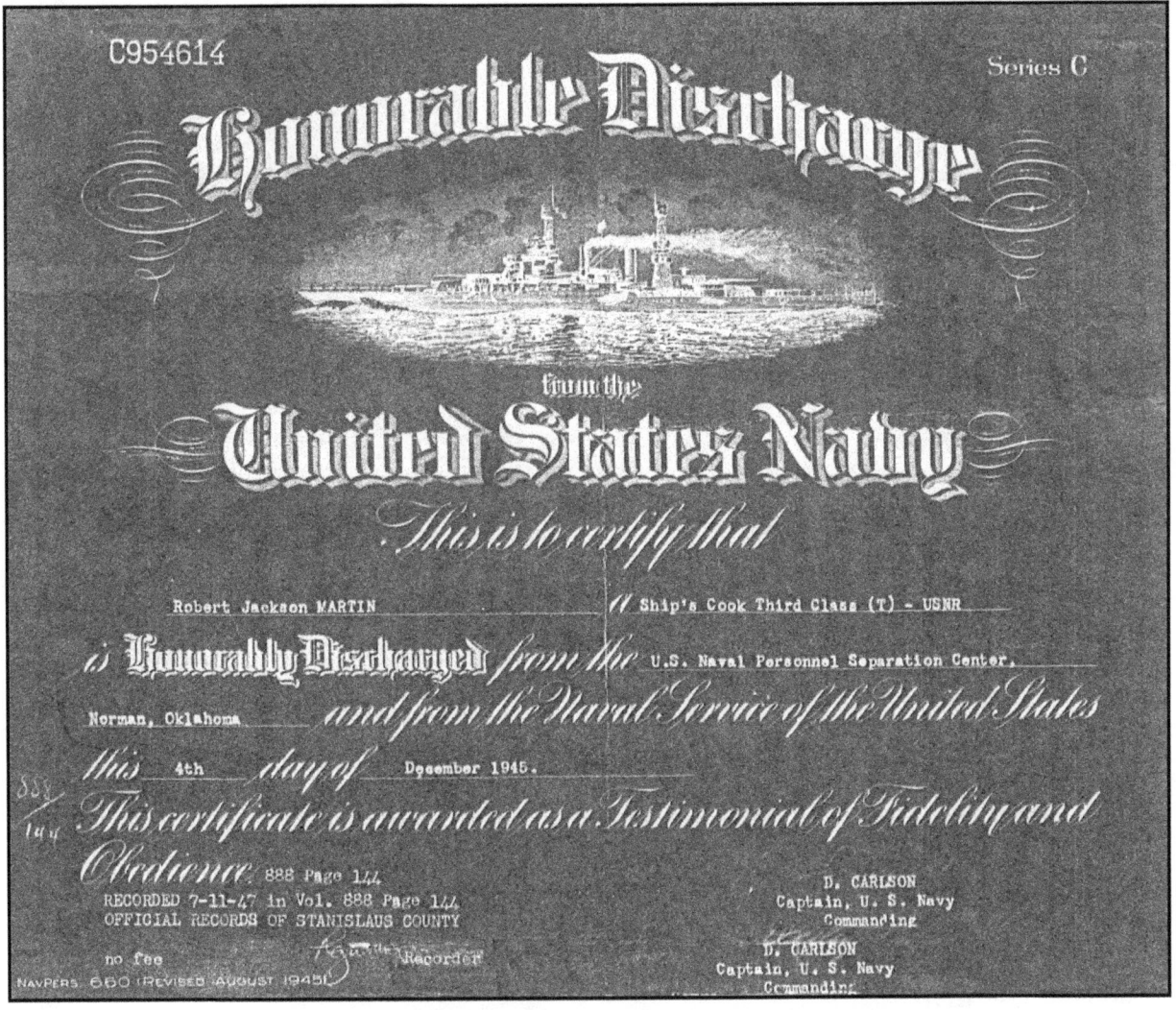

To serve bravely and proudly . . . and to make it home alive and well, honorably discharged from duty!

An Honorable Discharge from the United States Navy

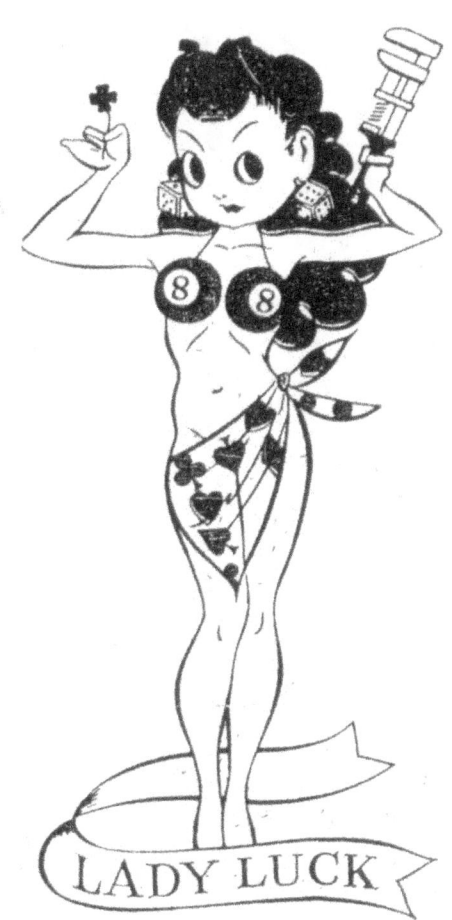

INDEX

A

Abderhalden, Ernest William . . . 21, 65, 90, 141

Adair, Richard Gale . . . 21, 46, 141

Adams, Charles Omer . . . 21, 23, 27, 141, 175

Adams, Harley Lee . . . 21, 23, 175

Alegarode, Sydney Cordell . . . 21

Allen, James D. . . . 27

Andrews, Fred C. . . . 27, 228, 231, 236

Andrews, Jean . . . 229, 234, 237

Ashton, Donald D. . . . 27

Augie . . . 48

B

Babineaux, Salamon . . . 27

Baerlin, Elmer E. . . . 27

Bailey, Howard E. "Buck" . . . 21, 42, 43, 52, 68, 80, 87, 111, 141

Balloons . . . 160

Barnes, Archie L. . . . 27

Barrage Balloons . . . 160

Barrow, William Bruce Jr. . . . 21, 142

Bartlett, Delmare Filmore . . . 21, 141

Basic Training . . . 17, 18

Basketball Team . . . 87

Battle Record on Conn . . . 68

Bauer, Dorothy . . . 221, 229, 234, 237

Bauer, Merle Floyd . . . 21, 47, 111, 126, 128, 220, 223, 225, 228, 230, 231, 236, 237, 239, 241

Bausman, Harold Lee . . . 46, 215, 220

Beach Party in the Philippines . . . 108

Belcher, Donald Arthur . . . 21

Belding, Croy Eugene . . . 21

Bell, Robert Louis . . . 21, 52, 103, 141

Bell, Walter Clarence . . . 21, 43

Bellis, Merle L. . . . 27

Benoit, Leon George . . . 21

INDEX

Berman, Raymond M. . . . 27

Berry, Francis T. . . . 27

Berry, Thomas Willard . . . 21

*Bertouille, Walter Edward
. . . 21, 51, 62, 70, 75, 102,
121, 141, 220, 225, 228*

*Berzinski, Roman "Breezy"
. . . 21, 62, 70, 80, 102, 111,
114, 126, 142, 220, 225, 228,
231, 233, 235, 236, 250, 251*

*Berzinski, Thelma . . . 70,
221, 227, 234, 237*

Bettys . . . 158, 182

*Bittiker, Harold Gene . . . 21,
39, 141, 175, 215*

Black Gang . . . 58, 90

Bowers, Floyd J. . . . 27

Boxers . . . 59

Branch, Eugene M. . . . 27

*Brandmair, Wilbur F. . . . 27,
76, 176, 252*

Broward, Montcalm III . . . 21

Browder, Robert W. . . . 27

*Brown, Charles Albert . . . 21,
54, 55, 56, 57, 188*

*Brown, Guile Fray . . . 21, 54,
55, 56, 57, 188*

*Buckingham, James Robert
. . . 21, 76, 77, 79, 141*

*Bullington, H. E. . . . 51, 66,
70, 102, 103, 104, 111, 114,
121, 141, 150, 250*

*Bunker, Frank . . . 21, 49, 50,
67, 93, 141, 252, 253*

*Burns, Eleanor . . . 221, 229,
234, 237*

*Burns, Francis J. "Frank"
. . . 27, 40, 42, 66, 70, 78, 80,
92, 102, 106, 111, 121, 125,
126, 130, 142, 213, 214, 220,
221, 222, 224, 225, 228, 230,
231, 233, 236, 237, 250*

☙ C ❧

*Caldie, John P. . . . 27, 220,
228*

Campbell, D. W. . . . 141

Cari, Robert R. . . . 27

Carlascio, William . . . 27

Carlton, Burnis P. . . . 27

Carlton, S. E. . . . 141

*Catholic Church Service in
Route to Okinawa . . . 77*

Chambless, E. P. . . . 90, 142

Charbless, Eugene . . . 21

China . . . 130

China Sea . . . 185

*Christening of LST-86
. . . 12, 15*

*Cleary, William Warner
. . . 21*

Collier, Vernon . . . 21

Cox, Thurman N. . . . 72, 142

INDEX

Crew Reunions . . . 213, 214

Crew Standing Inspection . . . 17

Crowell, Edward Belchner . . . 21, 141

Cruchfield, Fry Dovett Sr. . . . 21, 141

Crutchfield, J. D. . . . 21, 174

Cummins, Samuel Martin . . . 21

ଔ D ଋ

Denton, Jack Walton . . . 21, 40, 54, 57, 65, 121, 141

Dever, H. P. . . . 142

Deyer, Hugh Patrick . . . 21, 74, 77, 142

DiPalma, Andy J. . . . 21, 76, 125, 126, 141, 187

Dismon, John Bedford . . . 21, 65

Dobes, Frank William . . . 21, 47, 79, 141

Dobesh, Betty . . . 221, 229, 234, 237

Dobesh, Joseph George . . . 21, 23, 24, 27, 44, 78, 82, 99, 106, 141, 215, 220, 225, 228, 230, 231, 233, 235, 236, 252, 253

Dog Postcard . . . 93

Dorl, John R. . . . 27, 40

Dreese, M. . . . 142, 236

Dreese, Neva . . . 237

Dukman, Jerry Marvin Jr. . . . 21, 215

Dunman, J. M. Jr. . . . 21, 215

ଔ E ଋ

Ellis, Betty . . . 229

Ellis, David Nelson . . . 21, 42, 65, 66, 67, 101, 110, 142, 228, 231

Ellison, Cal -- LST-325 Memorial Fund . . . 239

Emmel, Donald John . . . 21, 77, 141, 215

Evans, James Haldon . . . 21, 27, 114, 141

ଔ F ଋ

Femrack, John Phillip . . . 21

Ferguson, Frank L. . . . 27

Ferraro, Johnny GM1c . . . 40, 77, 80

Ferrell, James M. . . . 27, 70, 175

Finn . . . 47

First Crew . . . 19-22

Flatt, Savage Dyer . . . 21, 141

Fry, Ernest Abraham . . . 21,

INDEX

40

Furnweger, Alfred J. . . . 27

ଓ G ଛ

Gainor, John Paul "Pops" . . . 21, 28-31, 131, 141, 253, 254

Galley of LST-864 . . . 106

Gay, David . . . 21, 48, 141

Gibson, B. Welbur . . . 20, 26, 35, 141, 228, 230, 231, 236, 241, 242

Gibson, Marge . . . 229, 237

Grady, C. R. . . . 19, 26

Granberry, Henry L. . . . 27

Gregg, Robert Leonard Jr. . . . 21, 98, 141

Guida, Arthur Joseph "Doc" . . . 21, 61, 175

ଓ H ଛ

Haines, F. Lee . . . 20, 23, 26, 32, 39, 141

Hammond, John Glenn . . . 21, 77, 215

Hanley, Eugene P. . . . 20, 26, 33, 34, 70, 72, 141, 214, 220, 225, 228, 231, 236, 246, 242

Hanley, Lolly . . . 237

Hanley, Mary . . . 237

Hanley, Peg . . . 237

Hanley, William R. . . . 20, 26, 33, 34, 70, 72, 77, 141, 214, 220, 225, 228, 231, 236, 246, 242

Harmon, Arthur Ross . . . 21, 90

Harp, Ted Jr. . . . 27

Harris, Harry . . . 231

History of the USS LST-864 . . . 177-185

Hock, Erwin Arthur . . . 21

Hogle, Paul Arnold . . . 21, 30, 142

Holland, J. W. . . . 20, 26, 37, 199

Holmes, James Richard . . . 21, 46, 82, 142

Holmes, L. P. Jr. . . . 20, 26, 141

Honorable Discharge . . . 256-257

Horner, Lewis Clinton . . . 21, 47, 59, 75, 141

Hughlin, James Hiram . . . 21

ଓ I & J ଛ

Jacobson, Gayle Carlo Martin . . . 21, 38, 39, 141, 150, 175, 215

Japanese Bettys . . . 158, 182

INDEX

Japanese Imperial Palace Grounds . . . 119, 126

Japanese Plane Crash . . . 119

Japanese Soldiers and Civilians . . . 122, 124, 125, 127, 128, 129

Japanese Sunken Ship . . . 115

Japanese Surrender . . . 247-249

Jeffersonville Boat and Machine ("Jeffboat") Company . . . 12, 14, 177, 189

Jensen, Harry Martin Sr. . . . 21

Jewell, Claude E. . . . 27, 220, 228, 231, 233, 236, 239

○ K ○

Kaehler, Malcolm Andrew "Freddie" . . . 21, 102, 141, 233, 234, 236, 237

Keeler, Loretta . . . 221, 229, 237

Keeler, Raymond E. . . . 27, 214, 220, 225, 228, 231, 236

Kidd, Frank C. . . . 27, 220, 236

Kidd, Gail . . . 237

Knapp, R. A. . . . 142

Knutson, Arthur Carl . . . 21, 39, 41, 69, 251

○ L ○

Lachey, Bruce N. . . . 27

Lady Luck . . . 84-86

Lady Luck Naming . . . 84-87

Langhett, Gerald LeRoy . . . 21, 73, 80

Lapham, Marvin James . . . 21, 41, 77, 142

Largent, Charles W. . . . 27

Larkin, Charles F. . . . 21, 30, 73

Launching of LST-864 . . . 12, 15, 16

Lawson, Romma Junior . . . 21

LCT-831 Loading/Unloading on LST-864 . . . 99, 118, 161

LCT-1428 Unloading . . . 100

Leake, John Glenn . . . 27

Leitl, Leo "Curly" . . . 73

Leverett, Garland Harold . . . 21, 142, 176

Lewis, Willie . . . 27

Leyte, the Philippines . . . 113

Lipinski, Beverly . . . 221, 234, 237

Lipinski, James Victor . . . 21, 48, 70, 80, 85, 104, 123, 125, 126, 127, 141, 214, 220, 225,

INDEX

228, 230, 231, 233, 235, 236, 239

Loar, Paul David . . . 21, 142

LST-6 . . . 211

LST-43 . . . 211

LST-69 . . . 211

LST-158 . . . 211

LST-167 . . . 211

LST-179 . . . 211

LST-203 . . . 211

LST-228 . . . 211

LST-282 . . . 211

LST-313 . . . 211

LST-314 . . . 211

LST-318 . . . 211

LST-325 Memorial Ship . . . 238, 239, 240, 241, 243, 244

LST-333 . . . 211

LST-342 . . . 211

LST-348 . . . 211

LST-349 . . . 211

LST-353 . . . 211

LST-359 . . . 211

LST-376 . . . 211

LST-396 . . . 211

LST-447 . . . 211

LST-448 . . . 211

LST-460 . . . 212

LST-472 . . . 212

LST-480 . . . 212

LST-493 . . . 212

LST-496 . . . 212

LST-499 . . . 212

LST-507 . . . 212

LST-523 . . . 212

LST-531 . . . 212

LST-563 . . . 212

LST-577 . . . 212

LST-675 . . . 212

LST-738 . . . 212

LST-749 . . . 212

LST-750 . . . 212

LST-808 . . . 212

LST-864 At Sea with a Movie Screen on Deck . . . 92, 161

LST-864 Captain's View of the Stern While at Sea . . . 191

LST -864 Crew Reunions . . . 213-244

LST-864 Departing the San Francisco Naval Yard . . . 88

LST-864 Docked at Midway . . . 82

LST-864 Empty Cargo Bay After Unloading . . . 97

INDEX

LST-864 Fully Loaded and Heading Out to Sea . . . 18, 45

LST-864 Galley . . . 106

LST-864 In San Francisco Bay . . . 188

LST-864 In the Panama Canal . . . 16

LST-864 Launching . . . 16

LST-864 Loading Cargo at a Dock . . . 94

LST-864 Mascots "LST-864" and "Chi Chi" . . . 32

LST-864 Naming . . . 84-88

LST-864 Trading Movies at Sea . . . 96, 132

LST-864 Unloading at Ie Shima . . . 115, 116

LST-864 Unloading at Pearl Harbor . . . 99, 100

LST-864 Unloading at Yokosuka . . . 118

LST-864 Unloading on a Beach . . . 106

LST-883 . . . 96

LST-906 . . . 212

LST-921 . . . 212

LST-1081 . . . 132

LST Defined . . . 11

LST Hull Schematics . . . 13

LST Sunk or Destroyed During WW II . . . 211, 212

Lyon, Malcolm Bernard . . . 21

○8 M 80

Magel (or Nagel), Sal M. . . . 22, 70

Maher, John N. . . . 41, 45, 64, 75, 142, 251

Mail Ship at Sea . . . 132

Majors, Charlie O. . . . 27, 72, 73

Marshall, Jesse Ray . . . 21

Martin, George Jackson . . . 255

Martin, Mary . . . 255

Martin, Robert Jackson . . . 18, 21, 49, 50, 53, 63, 188, 255, 256, 257, 258

Martinez, Salvador . . . 27, 185

Mascots--"LST-864" and "Chi Chi" . . . 32

May, Normal Call . . . 21, 176

McCloud, Nathaniel . . . 21, 71, 90, 141, 220, 253

McCloud, Priscilla . . . 221

McWhorter . . . 35

Memories of Captain Richard B. Wathen . . . 31, 189-210

Merriman, Lowall Arthur . . . 21

Michel, Willie J. . . . 27

INDEX

Miller, Betty . . . 237

Miller, Ronald Boyd . . . 21, 73, 80, 142, 236

Mitchell, Robart . . . 21, 90, 141

Mockbridge, Joseph Aleck . . . 21

Mosier, Milton Jr. . . . 27

Motes, J. H. . . . 182

Mother's Day Card . . . 131

Movie Screen on Ship . . . 161, 196

Mueller, Rose . . . 221, 229, 234, 237

Mueller, William Joseph . . . 21, 98, 141, 214, 215, 220, 225, 228, 230, 231, 233, 236, 239

Mullen, John Herman . . . 21, 142

Murray, Lawrence Ralph . . . 21

Myers, Herbert Benjamin . . . 21, 25, 74, 176

Nagel, Sal . . . 22, 70, 142

◊ N & O ◊

Naming of the Lady Luck . . . 84-88

Neal, Jack Lloyd . . . 21, 41, 141

Novak, Joseph . . . 27

O'Brien, Byron Francis . . . 21, 39, 46, 86, 142, 176

Okinawa . . . 185, 186, 187

Ostrem, Richard W. . . . 27

Outrigger Canoe . . . 108

◊ P & Q ◊

Page, Thomas A. . . . 27, 71

Parker, Ralph Wilbert . . . 21, 141

Parrick, LeRoy Junior . . . 21, 59, 79, 87, 102, 121, 141

Paulik, Joseph James . . . 21, 39, 65, 128, 142

Pearl Harbor . . . 105

Perry, Elderidge . . . 21, 62

Peter, Robert D. Jr. . . . 20, 26, 32, 36, 58, 62, 141, 246

Philippines . . . 107-113

Phillips, Richard . . . 27, 185

Pitts, Issac Newton Jr. . . . 21, 24, 37, 141, 176, 215, 216

Plonka, Alexander . . . 21, 141

Porter, Elmer . . . 5

Porter, Norman L. . . . 27, 252

Prokop, Andrew . . . 21, 59, 142

Provins, Geneva . . . 237

Provins, William Robert

INDEX

... 21, 56, 107, 141, 230, 236

Pyle, Ernie ... 95, 195

☙ R ❧

Radiomen ... 81

Reeble, William Keller Jr. ... 21, 142

Reed, Sue ... 221, 234, 237

Reed, William M. ... 27, 52, 185, 220, 225, 231, 235, 236, 244

Regel, Robert Christopher "Doc" ... 21, 61, 141, 176

Reunions ... 213, 214

Robins, William Hamilton ... 21, 142

Rogers, Richard F. ... 27

Rose, Glen Oval "Rosie ... 22, 52, 58, 130, 142, 150, 215

Rose (or Ross), Richard Claude ... 22, 39, 41, 174

Rushing, Walter O. ... 21, 23, 49, 79, 90, 142, 215, 216

Russell, Humphrey G. ... 27

Russell, Rodger Webb ... 21

☙ S ❧

San Diego Harbor, Philippines ... 107, 108

Sandage, Earl E. ... 174

Satterly, Lillard S. ... 21, 62, 68, 72, 142

Schuler, Albert Joseph ... 21, 90

Scott, John ... 174

Scuttlebutt ... 133-149

Second Crew ... 26-27

Shelton, James M. ... 21, 142

Ship's History ... 177-189

Ship's Mascot, "LST-864" ... 32

Smith, Clyde ... 174

Smith, Kenneth L. ... 27

Smith, Richard F. ... 27

Smolich, George ... 27

South China Sea ... 185, 186

Sowder, Jess ... 22

Spanky ... 47

Sparky ... 47

Storgaard, Chester Helm ... 21, 69, 75, 142

Stotts, Emery Eugene ... 21, 59, 141

Sunken Japanese Ship ... 115

Swazey, Leanard Willis ... 21, 42, 51, 62, 68, 70, 71, 80, 92, 102, 103, 104, 105, 111, 113, 114, 121, 142, 220,

INDEX

251

Swazey, Margaret . . . 221

Swope, Charlotte . . . 221, 229, 237

Swope, Julius Harold . . . 22, 70, 141, 215, 220, 228, 230, 231, 233, 236

Szersinski, Henry . . . 24, 72, 141

Szerzinski, Sylvester . . . 174

ଔ T ଞ

Tamulwich . . . 35

Tavron, M. C. . . . 27

Taylor, Robert V. . . . 27, 78

Terry, Aleene . . . 221, 229, 234

Terry, Joe Alexander "Doc" . . . 21, 61, 142, 176, 220, 225, 228, 230, 231

Thomas, Walter Evans . . . 21, 24, 30, 142, 175

Thompson, Ralph . . . 174

Thompson, Thurman N. . . . 21, 46, 74, 82, 142

Thompson, Tommy . . . 74, 82

Thompson, Willie L. . . . 27

Thurgo, Lyle E. . . . 27

Timpany, J. W. . . . 74, 121, 123, 124, 125, 141

Tinlin, Hubert Orton . . . 22, 30, 64, 142, 174, 215

Trading Films at Sea . . . 96

Truesdale, Vister Rutledge Jr. . . . 21, 48, 142

Typhoon . . . 151, 162-173, 206, 207

Typhoon Damage Report . . . 162-173

ଔ U - Z ଞ

Unnamed Crewmen . . . 24, 39, 40, 42, 43, 44, 46, 47, 49, 50, 53, 60, 62, 63, 64, 70, 73, 78, 79, 80, 81, 88, 98, 99, 102, 103, 104, 111, 113, 114, 119, 123, 173, 187, 188, 190, 228, 251

Utberg, C. A. Jr. . . . 52, 63, 141

VJ Day Celebrations . . . 250, 251, 252

Walczak, Leonard . . . 22, 49, 74, 114, 174

Walling, John W. . . . 27, 41, 44, 45, 64, 142

War Diary of LST-Group Ninety-One . . . 151-159

Warren, William K. . . . 27, 44, 175

Wartime Memories of Captain Richard B. Wathen . . . 189-210

Wathen, Richard B. . . . 19,

INDEX

20, 31, 89, 141, 189-210, 215, 216, 220, 221, 222, 223, 231, 235, 246

Wathen, Viola . . . 12, 15

Weather Balloons . . . 160

Wever, Darrell L. . . . 30, 64, 69, 75, 90, 142, 175

White, David "Wimpy" . . . 142, 236

White, Odd (Guest) . . . 236

White, Ova C. Jr. . . . 27, 38, 45

Whitehead, Clovie Armon . . . 21

Wick, Jean . . . 220, 221, 229, 234, 236, 237

Wick, Leander Norvert . . . 21, 64, 65, 66, 67, 101, 141

Wilder, J. W. Jr. . . . 27

Williams, J. W. . . . 26

Williams, John J. . . . 27

Wilson, William B. . . . 27

Winters, Charles Grandt . . . 21, 30, 64, 80, 142, 175

Wolbach, Paul W. . . . 21, 50

Womack, James Hubert . . . 22, 49, 141

Wood, Philip N. . . . 20, 23, 26, 28, 30, 35, 141

Wooster, L. P. . . . 141

Yokosuka, Japan . . . 118, 121, 123, 124, 125

Zorich, J. F. . . . 142

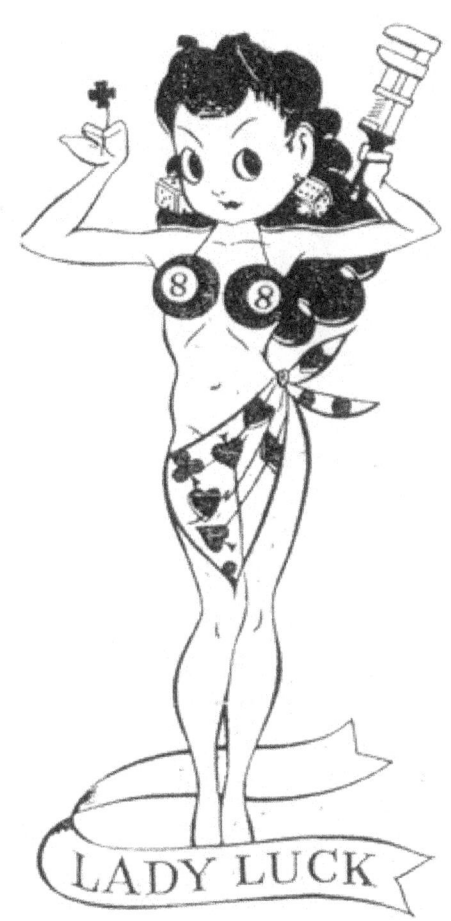

www.ingramcontent.com/pod-product-compliance
Lightning Source LLC
Chambersburg PA
CBHW080615170426
43209CB00007B/1440